Read People Like a Book

How to Speed-Read People, Analyze Body Language, and Understand Emotions

By: Discover Press

Table Of Contents

Introduction

You are walking down a city street on the way to work. You are startled when a strange man calls out to you and walks directly toward you. You do not know this man, so your first instinct is to assume he will ask you for money. At a closer look you notice that he is dressed sharply, he carries himself with confidence, and he has a disarming smile on his face. The man compliments you on your jacket. "Anyone that wears a jacket like this must have sophisticated taste," he says. You are pleased by the compliment—after all, you spent a whole hour shopping for this particular jacket—but you are also in a hurry to get to work. What exactly does this man want?

The man tells you his secret. He can read minds. You're skeptical, of course. Mind reading is a parlor trick reserved for so-called psychics or telepaths. Now you are convinced that this strange man is unwell. It is best to err on the side of caution and not upset him. You apologize and tell him you need to get to work. "Would you like me to teach you how to read minds?" he asks you. "I won't charge you a cent," the strange man says.

You can't help it, you're intrigued. You're not sure if this is an elaborate setup for a punchline or a sincere offer, but either way, your interest has been piqued. You consider for a moment; you weigh the pros and cons. Eventually, you realize that you just don't have the time for whatever silly game this man is playing. You're going to be late for work. You apologize to the man again, but you must go. "You don't believe me?"

the man says, "But I've been reading your mind this whole time!"

Now you've had it! Is this man claiming to know your innermost thoughts? What an invasion of privacy! But of course not. Mind reading is not real. This man is making claims that he can't back up. Now you feel your competitive nature rising from within you. You tell the man that if he can actually read your mind, then go ahead and prove it.

"Very well," the man says. "When I first called out, you braced your shoulders to protect your neck, so I read your mind as scared. After you saw me, you turned in my direction but scratched your neck, indicating you were uncertain of me. My compliment made you smile widely, and I read your mind to be proud of your taste. When I told you that I read minds you crossed and gripped your arms, indicating you were not buying what I was selling. When I offered to teach you how to read minds for free, you stroked your chin to indicate you were considering my offer, but you quickly sided against it and shook your head firmly. When I told you that I had been reading your mind the whole time, you pulled on your ear. You wanted to hear no evil; you did not believe me. Finally, you pointed directly at me when you demanded I prove myself, and I read your mind that you were looking to assert authority and make me listen."

You scoff at the man. He is very observant at best, but hardly a mind reader. Anyone could do what this strange man just did.

"Was I wrong?" the strange man asks.

The Importance of Reading People

This hypothetical anecdote gives us a solid foundation for the possibilities and limits of reading body language. There are many people who consider themselves experts on the subject of body language. They are scientists, psychologists, speech pathologists, FBI interrogators, and undercover agents, to name a few. None of these experts would proclaim themselves to be mind-readers.

Ask a friend to think of a number between 1 and 1000 and then try to guess their answer by reading their facial expression. Hopeless, right? Now say the name of a celebrity who you know your friend has strong feelings for. Were you able to pick up on your friend's feelings for that celebrity by watching the change in their facial expression? This is the important distinction between mind reading and evaluating body language. It might not be possible to literally read someone else's thoughts, but if you're insightful enough, you can make deductions on how someone is feeling based on their body language.

So, why is reading people so important? Great public speakers can read their audience and tell if they are attentively listening or growing bored. Expert salesmen can read potential customers and pick up on clues that there is something the customer is not telling them. Reading body language is just the half of it. Imagine if you could use that reading to then turn a bored crowd into a captivated audience, or a hesitant prospect into a decisive customer. That is where the real art of reading people lies.

Once you begin to understand how easy it can be to read people based on body language, you will begin to appreciate the magnitude of *your own* body language. Your body language can be the key to making a great first impression. It can be the difference between a disastrous first date and a lovely evening. It can be the reason why after you leave a job interview, your interviewer says to themselves, "I'm not sure why, but I really liked that candidate." Confidence, openness, and attentiveness are all attractive personality traits in new acquaintances, job candidates, and sexual partners. All of these attributes can easily be put on display with the right body language.

It turns out, the art of the conversation is less reliant on speech than it is on body language. This is a common theme throughout the academic study of body language that dates back to Charles Darwin's 1871 book: *The Expression of the Emotions in Man and Animals.* Darwin's theories were deeply rooted in biology and found startling similarities between the facial expressions of nonverbal animals and humans of all races. Later in the 1950s, an Iranian psychologist named Albert Mehrabian found that the impact of a message had very little to do with verbal communication. Mehrabian's findings indicated that a successful message relies on 7% spoken words, 38% vocal inflection and tone of voice, and 55% nonverbal communication. In other words, when you're trying to convince someone of something, the likelihood that you will succeed has 7% to do with the content of your speech, and 93% to do with how you say it.

There's no better way to test the importance of body language than to analyze the body language of famous people. Watch a famous movie star in one of their legendary roles. Haven't you ever wondered how a movie star can convey emotions so easily, often without any dialogue at all? This is because most movie stars are masters of body language. Go back to the days of Charlie Chaplin and Buster Keaton. These silent movie stars could not fall back on the spoken word to express emotions to their audience. It was all done through body language. Amazingly, the audiences never seemed to have trouble understanding what those mute stars were feeling. The same can be said of politicians, who are often trained in the art of body language. Politicians will often use expressions or mannerisms that let the audience know that they can be trusted. They will frequently gesture with open arms and palms, indicating that they are an open book and have nothing to hide. On the flipside, take a politician like Hitler, whose infamous palm-down salute was no accident—a downward palm is used to indicate your dominance over someone. This is not to say that politicians are experts at hiding their true feelings, because body language is often subconscious and impossible to hide. When Bill Clinton answered questions from a grand jury regarding Monica Lewinsky, he famously folded his hands, pressed his pointer fingers to his nose, and covered his mouth—a textbook sign of lying.

We should all strive to be fluent in body language. Body language is not just a helpful tool for reading people, but also for charming them. The social benefits of fine-tuned body language are exponential. Whether you're a social butterfly or an introverted loner, improving your body language skills can make an overwhelmingly positive impact on your life.

Why We Need to Connect

Human beings have a biological need to connect with each other. Ever since the dawn of man, humans have gathered in tribes in order to survive. There is strength in numbers. Nowadays our tribes look different than a pack of hunter-gatherers. Our tribes are our families, our communities, our classrooms, our group of friends, or our coworkers, to name a few. When we interact within our tribes, we are stimulating our brains. Social stimulus gives us just as big of a dopamine hit as any drug. Loving messages from family members, laughter from a friend, or praise from a boss can all be deeply rewarding feelings.

There are also social and psychological benefits to meeting new people. No matter how scared you are of meeting new people, the science behind the benefits is hard to ignore. Studies have found that people with strong social ties have longer lifespans. In a 1979 study by Dr. Lisa Berkman, 7,000 people ages 35 to 65 were examined over the course of nine years. It was found that the subjects with little to no social contacts were three times more likely to die of medical illness than the subjects with extensive contacts. These are eye-opening findings, especially considering that genetics, socioeconomic status, and pre-existing health factors did not affect the results of the study.

You've likely heard the expression "It's all about who you know." Building your own personal network is a fantastic way to set yourself up for success down the line. You never know when you might need to call on someone in your network for a favor, and the more people in your network you have, the more people you can turn to. The social benefits of having a large network may seem obvious, but biologically, it also gives us a feeling of safety. This safety can have a vast positive impact on your mental and physical well-being.

Human beings also need emotional and sexual relationships. Nothing can be more rewarding than having a close and intimate relationship with your partner. Giving and receiving love is a biological necessity just as much as food and water. Granted, it is not always easy. Managing a long-term relationship will never be a cakewalk. Communication is key. So why does communication between husband and wife so often fall apart?

If social connections are essential, it would make sense to accumulate as many new friends and acquaintances as possible. If emotional relationships are needed, then it stands to reason you should try hard to foster those relationships. Perhaps there is nothing you can do to help yourself. Some people are likable and popular. Some people are naturally empathetic. Some people lack the emotional understanding to take a friendship or marriage the distance. But is it really that simple? Or is there a secret to connecting with people?

In this book, we will explore how body language is the secret behind not just reading people but connecting with and understanding them. Reading and analyzing people is not just a cheap parlor trick; it can be the difference between a failed relationship or a healthy one. Walk into any room of people and make a great first impression. Recognize when something is bothering your friend. Notice when you are beginning to drive your spouse crazy. These are skills that every human can benefit from.

Once you have garnered a better understanding of body language, you will likely find that you're more emotionally conscious of your loved one's feelings. You will become more aware of the impact your words and actions have on others. You will less easily be duped by people who offer empty promises.

Reading body language is an art that anyone can learn. There is no special gift required. Nor does special training come into play. All human beings use certain body language and facial expressions that translate to mean the same thing. Sometimes humans consciously convey messages using body language, other times the messaging is sent completely subconsciously. With enough practice, you'll be able to tell what someone is feeling, even when they think they are being coy. If you study the patterns enough, soon you will be able to speak the language. The truth is, no matter how good any of us think we are at hiding our emotions, most of us can be read like a book.

Emotional Intelligence

Creatures of Emotion

Before we can dig into the nuances of body language, we must first delve into what it is that drives people to act in a certain way. We unintentionally and unknowingly reveal the way we feel through our body language. We have next to no control over our emotions and our body's response to these emotions. When we are sad, we cry. When we are happy, we smile. There is rarely a conscious decision behind these reactions. Think of body language as a window into a person's emotions.

Human beings are complex creatures. On one hand, you have thoughtful beings that are capable of complex intellectual theory; rational organisms that are capable of problem-solving under immense pressure. On the other hand, you have irrational creatures that are governed by emotion; mammals that act under the influence of unconditional love, jealousy, attraction, anger, and every other human emotion that defies reason. When a parent steps in front of an oncoming car to shield their child, when a man has an affair with his brother's fiancée, or when a scorned lover commits a crime of passion, it's hard to believe that reason came anywhere into play. These are acts of emotion, pure and simple.

So, when exactly do humans put their rational thought to use? How about voting? Think again. Numerous studies have shown that voters pick their candidate based on a wide variety of emotional factors, but it rarely has anything to do with rationality. People vote based on their biases. If a voter believes a candidate shares values with themselves, they are likely to overlook policy in favor of values. Voters are also superficial. If the voter feels the candidate looks and sounds like a leader, they will likely cast their ballot in favor of that candidate. Perhaps you've heard of the beer test as a bellwether for picking presidents. This age-old question of what candidate you'd rather have a beer with sounds like a completely irrational thing to consider when picking what president to vote for, but then again, irrationality is often what drives humans to action.

Hundreds of studies have been conducted that lend credence to the theory that human beings make decisions based on emotions. Salesmen and women can often be heard repeating the mantra: "People buy on emotions and justify with logic." Statistically, this is true. Up to 90% of decisions are made based on emotion, according to studies.

It would seem that human beings, although they have the ability to be rational, are motivated first and foremost by emotion. Much like picking candidates, our feelings toward people we have just met are often irrational. The reason first impressions are so important is because we humans like to be correct. If we meet someone new and are sufficiently charmed, our brains will look to confirm this intuition with every subsequent meeting. This is called a confirmation bias and is just one of many biases that trick the brain into believing it is behaving rationally.

Human beings are creatures that make impulsive decisions, take shortcuts, and jump to conclusions. The reason this is the case is because without impulse, shortcuts, and jumping to conclusions, humans would shut down due to sensory overload. We would be unable to accomplish even the most menial tasks. Quick emotional decisions are essential to human function. You do not have to think analytically before deciding whether you should step out into oncoming traffic or wait for the cars to stop for pedestrians. It doesn't require laborious rational thought to come to the conclusion that you should not touch a hot stove. The exercise of critical thinking is a tiresome task for humans, and thus we use shortcuts to reduce stress and preserve our sanity. Emotional decision-making is not so much a flaw of human design as it is an evolutionary survival technique.

Thus, when human beings interact, they rely on surface-level clues to understand each other. Every human being reads body language, whether they are conscious of it or not. It is a shortcut, to be sure, but often a deadly accurate shortcut.

Leading with Empathy

It stands to reason that if you can understand human emotions, you can understand human body language, and vice versa. A disciplined student in the intricacies of other people's emotions can be said to possess high *emotional intelligence* (EQ). Unlike IQ, emotional intelligence is hard to define. Think of emotional intelligence as the ability to identify emotion in yourself and others.

Empathy is the trait most often associated with emotional intelligence. The ability to put yourself in someone else's shoes and understand their emotions is an invaluable skill to possess. But empathy alone is not enough. The key to

11

empathy is self-awareness. The more honest we are with ourselves about our feelings, the more apt we will be at recognizing feelings in others.

So how do we identify emotions in people? How are others able to identify our emotions? People rarely come out and tell you how they are feeling. Most people do not enjoy talking about feelings, except perhaps with their therapist. The majority of empathetic intuition comes from nonverbal cues (i.e., body language).

One of the most influential studies on the topic of nonverbal cues was conducted by Robert Rosenthal in 1979. Rosenthal developed what he coined the PONS test (Profile of Nonverbal Sensitivity) and administered it to over seven thousand subjects. The test involved showing subjects a series of videotapes of a woman displaying various nonverbal cues such as gratitude, seduction, anger, and affection. The areas of the body that were depicted in the video varied, sometimes only showing hand motion, and other times only showing facial tics. Other videos included muffled words with no video, to see if subjects could detect the correct emotion simply from the tone of voice. The design of this test was meant to determine the ability of the subjects to correctly empathize with others based on specific nonverbal cues.

The results of the PONS test were quite definitive. There was a direct correlation between having a strong ability to read nonverbal cues (having high emotional intelligence) with success in life. Test subjects who scored high on the PONS test were found to be more popular, well-adjusted emotionally, more outgoing, and more sensitive. Now here's the interesting part: there was only an incidental relationship between strong emotional intelligence and IQ. Young students who tested well on the PONS test proved to be the most emotionally stable, popular, and successful in their schools. They even did better in school than their classmates with higher IQs, but lower emotional intelligence. It would seem that emotional intelligence is just as valuable as IQ.

Empathy is something that develops extremely early in infancy. This fact reveals just how innate and essential empathy is to understanding others. It is a skill we've been developing since we were mere months old. Infants. Researchers have pointed to the response of newborn babies who become upset when they hear another baby crying. At such an early age, it is most likely that the infant does not even comprehend autonomy; they do not understand that another baby's suffering is not their own. And yet, they understand the feeling of suffering, and so they cry at the sound of another baby crying. This is an example of *motor mimicry*: an early stage of empathy.

One of the most powerful ways for a young child to develop their emotional intelligence is through *attunement*. Attunement is the process of a child finding validation for their emotions through others, most often their parents. If a baby is excited and happy, it is looking for a reciprocated level of emotion from their parent. If a baby squeals with delight, it is looking for a playful and happy face from their parent. When a parent matches their baby's emotion and lets the baby know that their emotion is shared, the baby feels emotionally connected. Alternatively, if a baby often squeals with delight and is routinely ignored by their parents, the baby will learn not to express these outward displays of happiness because it does not successfully gain the attention of their parents. Severe mis-attunement within a child's upbringing can lead to depleted emotional intelligence as they grow older.

The progression of empathy is often quite visible as a child grows older. After one year of age, the child begins to recognize their autonomy and understand that a crying baby's suffering is separate from their own. A child might now try and comfort the crying infant by offering them their teddy bear, something that they turn to when they are upset. By age two, children will begin to realize that all unpleasant emotions are not the same, and offering their teddy bear up as comfort might not be a solution to someone else's misery. Later in childhood, empathy advances to the point where children can feel pity for a whole group of people, such as the poor or sick.

As we grow older, empathy and EQ become pivotal tools at our disposal. They help us make friends, maintain relationships, and succeed at our jobs. Studies have shown that EQ accounts for 58% of performance at all jobs. If you possess high emotional intelligence, it can be reasonably predicted that you will achieve excellence in your personal life and career.

Now that we have established that empathy and EQ are essential elements of understanding emotion, why should you care? The answer is simple. IQ has proven to be stagnant and unchangeable. Your IQ is defined as your ability to learn, and that ability is fixed at birth. EQ, on the other hand, can be developed and refined. You are not born with a set limit of emotional intelligence. This means that through practice and discipline you can greatly increase your EQ.

In 2001, Drs. Travis Bradberry and Jean Greaves developed a test that could measure EQ called the Emotional

Intelligence Appraisal. Their findings have broken new ground in how people understand EQ. Bradberry and Greaves tested over 500,000 subjects for their groundbreaking research. The most telling finding of their studies might be this: only 36% of tested subjects could accurately identify their emotions as they occurred. This is a large deficit of people who suffer from suboptimal emotional intelligence; a wide-open competitive advantage for individuals who are high in EQ.

Using the Bradberry and Greaves model, we will explore the skills and strategies that can help someone improve their EQ.

How to Improve Emotional Intelligence

According to Bradberry and Greaves, there are four skills that make up the framework for an individual's EQ. They are self-awareness, self-management, social awareness, and relationship management. Let's examine each of these skills separately and unpack exactly what it means to be skilled in each of these areas.

Self-Awareness

Self-awareness is the ability to understand your inner workings. People who possess the ability to recognize and analyze their emotions are high in self-awareness. All of us think and behave in certain patterns, and once you understand the patterns you follow, you are well-positioned to utilize these patterns to your benefit. What incentivizes you? What makes you frustrated? How do you behave under stress? Questions such as these are important to achieving self-awareness.

High self-awareness can be difficult to attain because it involves taking a hard internal look at yourself and coming to grips with what makes you tick. Reflecting on your emotions and their roots is often an uncomfortable experience for people. It is much easier to simply never question your impulses and feelings and live a life of ignorant bliss. However, lacking self-awareness can be a major detriment to your social, romantic, and professional life. People who lack self-awareness are oblivious to how their words and actions affect the people around them. It is no wonder that people who lack self-awareness have trouble holding onto jobs and staying in healthy relationships.

Studies show that 83% of people that are high in self-awareness are top performers in their given field, while only 2% of people at the bottom of their field are found to be high in self-awareness. People that know themselves well have a good grasp of their strengths and weaknesses. They will choose career paths that suit them and give them an opportunity to flourish. They are also more equipped to objectively look at their performance and determine how they can improve. Being self-aware is not about being hypercritical of yourself; to be self-aware means that you are not afraid of your emotions. If you receive a scorching review from your boss, you can take it personally and convince yourself that you are a terrible employee, or you can use your self-awareness to identify the skills that can help you utilize the feedback and improve your performance. This is the difference between employees with low and high self-awareness.

As part of their study into emotional intelligence, Bradberry and Greaves reviewed job evaluations for test subjects and compared the evaluations of individuals who tested high in self-awareness against the individuals who tested low. They found that employees with similar self-awareness scores tended to receive a lot of the same feedback from supervisors. Employees who tested high in self-awareness were said to be "in charge of their emotions," "calm and collected," as well as "confident." These employees were open and honest about their emotions, thus quickly able to gain the trust of their team. Conversely, employees with low self-awareness were described as "insensitive," "defensive/aggressive," or "oblivious." These individuals were unaware of how they made their coworkers feel, which often caused unnecessary stress to be inflicted on their team members. Bosses that make their employees feel insecure, subordinates that are unwilling to accept criticism, and employees that are unknowingly rude to customers are all classic examples of workers with low self-awareness.

So how can you improve your self-awareness? You can start by carving out a minimal amount of time in your day to reflect on your recent emotions and how you responded to them. Self-awareness comes from within. Try analyzing the way you're behaving while completely reserving judgment. It may be impossible to eliminate emotions from our lives, but the first step in controlling your emotions is understanding them. When you think about your feelings, stop labeling them as good or bad. There are no such things as good or bad feelings. All emotions reveal some element of truth about ourselves. By quickly labeling a feeling as good or bad, you learn to enjoy the "good" feelings and hate the "bad" ones, while never really being aware of what the feeling is trying to tell you. This cheapens a feeling's significance. Next time you are experiencing a powerful feeling, don't simply enjoy or hate it, but take the time to discover what that feeling is trying to tell you.

Another useful tool for building self-awareness is to keep a journal of your emotions. Writing something down gives it a greater impact on your mind. It also allows you to revisit your past emotions and recognize patterns. Write down things that you notice make you annoyed, or how your words affected those around you, or how you felt while watching a movie. It can seem trivial, but journaling about the most mundane aspects of your day might reveal something about yourself that you never noticed.

Improving your self-awareness is all about embracing discomfort. Burying emotions deep inside might be easier in the short term, but it will always come back to bite you in the long term. These buried emotions will often reveal themselves in unintended ways and could negatively impact those around you. Being willing to explore emotions as they occur instead of burying them for later is a true gift of self-awareness. In order to improve your self-awareness, you must be willing to do some uncomfortable soul searching. You will reap the rewards, and you will find that it is not as painful as you feared it might be.

Finally, one of the most valuable skills of a highly self-aware individual is to not be fooled by your emotions. Riding the high of a good mood or falling into the pit of a bad mood leads to poor decision-making. We all go through shifts in our mood and recognizing a shift can allow you to avoid the typical traps of a mood. When you are in a good mood, you see green lights everywhere you go, and you might miss obvious warning signs that you need to slow down. On the other end of the spectrum, a bad mood can cloud your judgment and cause you to see everything in a negative light. The more objective you can be about your moods, the more likely you can eliminate their effect on your decision-making.

Self-awareness is a common skill of any emotionally intelligent individual. It is an area of personal competence that increases your ability to not only function but to excel in your life. Next, we will explore another skill that falls under the category of personal competence: self-management.

Self-Management

Simply put, self-management is your ability to execute on your self-awareness. As we have established, self-awareness is the skill of recognizing and understanding your emotions. Self-management is how you use this understanding to your benefit. Self-management is the action side of personal competence. You may be self-aware enough to know that when your spouse asks you a lot of questions, you become annoyed and rude. Self-management is what will help you keep your emotions in check and avoid turning innocuous questions into a blowout fight.

Self-management is not just the act of controlling your emotions. It is also the discipline of forsaking temporary needs in pursuit of long-term goals. In this sense, self-management can be developed with the help of daily habits. Everyone knows someone that is well organized and detail oriented. These are not genetic traits inherited at birth, but rather skills that are honed over time with self-management. Even though you might think you completely lack self-management, everyone has at least a small amount of self-management. When you get a terrible night's sleep and wake up on the wrong side of the bed, do you go back to sleep and play hooky from work? The short-term satisfaction of sleeping in and missing work might feel nice, but most people have the self-management to know that the long-term impact of this decision (potentially losing your job) is not worth the few hours of extra sleep.

Almost everyone who has worked a job has encountered a stressful day of work. When stress builds up and pressure mounts, the correct course of action is often unclear. Emotions can get the better of us, and they might even attempt a hostile takeover and cause a shutdown. People with high self-management skills always seem to handle high-pressure situations calmly and make them look easy. This has nothing to do with their ability to always see the right course of action. High self-management skills do not cause you to always make the right choice. Self-management will allow you to embrace the uncertainty of a high-pressure situation and not let your emotions take control. If you skillfully manage your emotions in these stressful situations, you will be in much better shape to make a well-informed and rational decision.

Employees with high self-management scores are able to communicate directly and honestly with their team members. They do not succumb to the temptation of getting emotional in a stressful situation. While some employees in the office might not be able to work together due to a "personality clash," a high self-management individual can work with anyone and can tailor their communication style to different team members. A customer service rep who calmly and politely speaks with an irate customer can be said to have strong self-management skills. Employees who lack self-management skills are reactive instead of proactive. They are quick to get emotional and say or act in a way that adds stress to everyone's work environment. Low self-management is the reason why some people are constantly at the mercy of their emotions.

Achieving self-management in your life is a huge part of emotional intelligence. People that appear to be controlled by their emotions are often frustrating to be around. Outbursts of anger, irrational decisions, and unnecessary rudeness are all terrible traits to exhibit if you are looking to be a top performer at your job or maintain a relationship with a significant other. Fortunately, there are quite a few practical strategies you can implement that can help with your self-management.

Some of the most useful techniques for improving self-management sound trite, but that does not mean they do not work. Proper breathing is one such technique. You have no doubt heard the expression, "take a deep breath." There is hard science behind this expression. Twenty percent of the oxygen you breathe in is used by the brain. The brain needs a healthy amount of oxygen in order to function at a high level. If you have a habit of taking short and shallow breathes all day, it is likely you are not getting enough oxygen to your brain. A lack of oxygen to the brain will lead to a lack of concentration, mood swings, and anxiety, among other things.

Another such technique is to count to ten. When emotions get the best of you, you are likely to speak or act impulsively. This should be avoided when possible. Patience is a huge part of self-management. Stopping what you are doing and slowly counting to ten in your head will help settle you down. Taking nice deep breaths as you count are recommended as well.

A strong sleep schedule is another helpful habit to develop. When you operate on an unhealthy amount of sleep, you are going to be hampered by a clouded mind. Your brain needs sleep to recharge and feel fresh for the next day. Try to instill consistency into your sleep schedule so that you can teach your body at what time it should expect sleep. If you are someone who historically has trouble falling asleep, you may need to examine some of your habits that could be causing your insomnia. Try cutting out caffeine as much as possible. Caffeine has a six-hour half-life, which means that if you drink a coffee at 8 AM, you will still have 25% of that caffeine in your bloodstream when it is time for bed. Over exposure to your phone or laptop screen can also be harmful to your sleep schedule. The light from screens tricks your brain into thinking you are being exposed to sunlight, which in turn makes your body think it is daytime. Try putting away your phone and laptop an hour before bed.

Perhaps the most important strategy for self-management is the ability to control your *self-talk*. It is said that the average human experiences 50,000 unique thoughts a day. Each of these thoughts will trigger a corresponding emotion. Think of this constant barrage of thoughts that you are experiencing as "self-talk." The best thing you can do for yourself is to practice the art of positive self-talk. Negative self-talk can lead to insecurity, oversensitivity, and unhealthy self-criticism. Next time you make a mistake, don't tell yourself "I'm an idiot," but rather tell yourself "I made a mistake." Eliminate the words "always" and "never" from your self-talk arsenal. When you let your emotions get the best of you, tell yourself "I got emotional this time," but do not tell yourself "I always get emotional." This practice will go a long way to improving your self-management mindset.

Now that we have explored the skills of self-awareness and self-management, we have covered the personal competency aspect of emotional intelligence. Next, we will dive into the social competency field.

Social Awareness

Social awareness is the skill of emotional intelligence that most closely ties in with the topic of this book: body language. Social awareness is your ability to pick up on social cues and understand the emotions of others. To be skilled at social awareness, one must be an observant onlooker and thoughtful listener. When you are in a conversation with someone, are you truly taking in everything they are telling you, or are your thoughts going elsewhere? If they are uncomfortable with a conversation topic you have broached, can you sense this, or are you going to continue to upset them?

The people with the highest social awareness have a gift for attunement. As we covered earlier in this chapter, attunement is the concept of understanding emotions in others, matching the emotions, and thus validating those emotions. When we are visibly upset about something (for example, the death of a relative), we might be offended by someone acting carefree around us, because this suggests that they are oblivious to our feelings. Someone who makes an inappropriate joke at a work function is someone that lacks basic social awareness.

Employees who test high in social awareness have been found to be astute readers of emotions within their teammates. They show that they have a genuine interest in the people they work with through meaningful conversations. They are respectful and they know how to communicate professionally. A supervisor with strong social awareness can sense that something is bothering one of their subordinates without them saying so. Social awareness is also one of the most important traits of a great leader. Social awareness can help you be inspiring and motivating to others.

An employee who suffers from low social awareness might be impatient and unsympathetic to others' issues. They are quick to shoot ideas down and are oblivious to how their coworkers feel. Those that lack social awareness are typically poor listeners, which leads to miscommunications often. Coworkers are likely to be put off by people with low social awareness because they come off as apathetic.

To become skilled at the art of social awareness, you need to train yourself to always watch for body language. We delve much deeper into the intricacies of body language further into this book, but it is an essential part of social awareness. Once you have learned to read someone through their body language, you put yourself in a position to easily empathize and communicate with that person.

One easy trick to apply in any social setting is to call someone by their name. Research has shown that you receive a small hit of dopamine when you hear your name. Saying someone's name in a conversation will help create a positive impression in that person's mind. Always greet people by their name if you can. It's a simple and easy way to make the person you are conversing with feel special and seen.

Another aspect of social awareness is the concept of proper timing. There always a time and a place for a conversation, but starting a conversation in the wrong setting could be very off-putting. If your boss is venting to you about the inefficiency of his superiors, it might not be the right time to ask for that raise. Strategic timing is all about recognizing the mood of the people around you and acting in accordance with their mood. Perhaps you have heard the expression "read the room." If your timing is poor, you might come off as insensitive to those around you.

While listening is a huge part of social awareness, oftentimes people might not talk to you unless they are primed. Asking questions is one of the most vital tricks in a socially aware person's repertoire. If you suspect that someone is upset about something but you are not sure, just ask them. If you are not sure if you understood the person talking, ask them to clarify. You can say, "If I understand you correctly..." and then relay back to them what you believe their feelings to be. This is an excellent way to make people feel understood and heard.

We will explore more tips and tricks for increasing social awareness in later chapters. Building up your body language literacy is one of the best ways to increase social awareness. Next, we will delve into the last EQ skill: relationship management.

Relationship Management

Relationship management is someone's ability to skillfully navigate the emotions of themselves and others to have a successful interaction. It can also be characterized as the strength of the bond that you build with someone over time. People with strong relationship management skills often have a large network of people that they can rely on. They are also exceptional at gaining the trust of others and communicating important messages.

All relationships require work, some more than others. Marriage is a relationship that requires constant work and sacrifice to make it last. Obviously, most relationships don't require as much effort to maintain, but all of the aspects of a strong marriage can also be seen in any successful relationship. You need to be willing to listen, to share, and to make yourself available to the other person. Nothing is more valuable than time. When you go out of your way to give someone your time, you are expressing to them that you value their relationship. This is why the people we communicate with the most are usually the people we are closest with.

Job evaluations of people with strong relationship management skills have revealed that they are almost always excellent communicators. People with high relationship management scores are known to be reliable. They frequently exhibit signs that they have respect for their coworkers. Nonjudgmental listening skills, willingness to help, and eagerness to take a personal interest in others are all common signs that a person has good relationship management skills.

Individuals who test much lower in the area of relationship management are often found to view relationships as one-sided. If they do not feel that a relationship would be beneficial to them, they have no interest in putting in the time or effort. Bosses that have poor relationship management skills will likely butt heads with many of their subordinates. It is also likely that they will pick favorites and invest highly in certain relationships while investing nothing in others. This can lead to a strained work environment. People who struggle with relationship management likely struggle with the idea of tailoring communication styles based on who they are talking to. Not everyone has the same style and opinions, and people with strong relationship management skills recognize this.

One way in which you can improve your relationship management is by practicing clear and concise communication. Leading with honesty is a great way to gain trust and establish a connection with someone. If you are making a decision in the workplace that affects the team, let them know the rationale behind your decision. The more open and honest you are, the easier it will be for others to relate to you.

One specific way in which you can practice honest communication with others is to avoid sending mixed signals. As we know, body language often reveals the truth even when our words are telling a lie. If you are giving someone an insincere compliment, it is possible that your body language or voice pitch is giving away the truth. You would be surprised at how often people (including yourself) pick up inconsistencies between body language and speech. These inconsistencies will leave a bad taste in people's mouths. That is why it is wise to always be honest. Instead of giving an insincere compliment, try finding something else that you can complement someone for. Don't risk sending mixed signals that leave people with bad impressions.

Acknowledging other people's feelings is a great way to maintain a strong relationship. Vocalizing that you recognize and understand someone's emotions will make them feel seen and prove that you are someone that cares. Matching people's emotional level with attunement is a great strategy for making connections, but there are times when this won't work. Sometimes someone might be feeling something completely unique to themselves based on a personal situation, and the best thing you can do is acknowledge their feelings and listen.

Finally, a great relationship management tool is to face difficult conversations head-on. You should never try to avoid the inevitable. If there is something that is going unsaid within a relationship, by not addressing it, all you are doing is allowing it to fester. Once you begin the practice of proactively tackling difficult conversations, you will find that it is remarkably helpful for building the foundations of a solid relationship. Do your best to see the other person's perspective and try your hardest to clearly articulate your side. You will find that the relationship has grown stronger due to your willingness to talk out your issues.

A truly emotionally intelligent person is well versed in all four of the EQ skills: self-awareness, self-management, social awareness, and relationship management. All four of these skills cover a wide variety of human interactions. They help us to understand people, as well as ourselves. Emotionally intelligent people have been proven to find more success in life. The EQ skills can be learned, they can be improved, and they can be mastered. Anyone that is interested in the art of reading people must first learn how people feel. We are all emotional creatures, and we are all susceptible to the charms of emotionally intelligent individuals.

Personality Types

Myers-Briggs

In the last chapter, we discussed emotional intelligence and the similarities between human beings. All humans are emotional creatures, and everyone falls somewhere on the spectrum of EQ. We also examined some of the evergreen strategies that can be used to improve your personal and social competencies. However, we did not discuss the differences in human beings. In this chapter, we will do just that.

It is true that every human being is unique. No two people share the same DNA. Yet, it would not be true to say that every human being has their own unique personality. Personality comes from a combination of genes, upbringing, culture, time period, and location. A person's personality determines how they will act in a given situation. It determines their preferences and values. It determines strengths and weaknesses. Unlike emotional intelligence, personality is not indicative of success in your lifetime. However, someone's personality type can tell us a whole lot about a person.

One of the most famous personality tests is the Myers-Briggs Type Indicator. This famous test labeled sixteen different personality types that an individual could fall into based on various factors. This test proved to be a very useful tool for understanding people and speed-reading them. Based on where a person falls within the Myers-Briggs Type Indicator, they are likely to behave in a similar way as others that fall within the same personality category. If you know someone's personality type, it is a huge advantage in your ability to read them.

The Myers-Briggs test includes a total of sixteen personalities that are broken up into four dimensions. Each dimension is a scale that includes two endpoints on opposite ends of the spectrum. These dimensions are:

- **How People Are Energized: Extraversion (E) vs. Introversion (I)**
- **The Kind of Information We Naturally Pay Attention To: Sensing (S) vs. Intuition (N)**
- **How We Make Decisions: Thinking (T) vs. Feeling (F)**
- **How We Like to Organize Our World: Judging (J) vs. Perceiving (P)**

Each personality type includes one endpoint from each of the four dimensions. For example, an ESTJ is an extroverted person who senses information, thinks about decisions, and judges the world. While this framework is a simplified version of the spectrum of human personality, it is a useful tool for categorization.

Extraversion (E) vs. Introversion (I)

Extroverts are often thought to be gregarious social butterflies, while introverts are shy misanthropes, but this is a vast oversimplification. The real distinction between the two is where they draw their energy from. Extroverts draw their energy from other people, while introverts draw their energy from being alone. Another way to frame it is that extroverts are energized by people and things, while introverts are energized by ideas and thoughts.

Extroverts tend to focus on the world around them. Conversely, introverts tend to prefer time spent alone so they can focus on their thoughts. Extroverts tend to be impulsive people that enjoy getting involved with several projects that are going on at the same time. Introverts are overthinkers that tend to focus on one project at a time.

Of the four dimensions, extroverts and introverts are the easiest to identify in others. You can just meet someone for the very first time and have a good idea as to whether they are introverted or extroverted. Introverted are more reserved in their body language, they speak quieter, and their demeanor is calmer. Extroverts, on the other hand, will often use expressive hand gestures, and a wide array of facial expressions. When you read someone's body language, try to determine if the person favors big, animated gestures compared to more subtle and reserved ones. This will be the quickest way to determine if someone is an introvert or extrovert.

The next time you are in a group setting such as a party, take a mental itinerary of the guests. Who are the people that are the most social? The ones that seem to be gaining energy from the more people they talk to? Those are your extroverts. Who are the ones that are finding a quieter area of the party or having individual conversations? These are your introverts.

Extroverts grow uncomfortable in silence. When they are asked a question, they will often answer immediately because they do not want to leave any dead air. Introverts are more likely to pause and think when they are asked a question.

For introverts, silence is not awkward; at times it is even preferred. Introverts are much less likely than their extroverted counterparts to speak up and break a silence.

Extroverts often get a reputation for taking over a conversation, especially when talking with an introvert. While extroverts have no problem speaking up and making small talk, that does not mean they are the only talkers. A good tip-off that you might be talking to an extrovert is if they begin to speak up and dominate a conversation when it is something they are particularly passionate about.

Sensing (S) vs. Intuition (N)

The second dimension has to do with how people perceive information. The way we view the world determines on which side of this spectrum we fall. Sensors tend to be detail-oriented people that use their five senses to take in information. Intuitive people, on the other hand, are more imaginative and often make connections while searching for the underlying meaning of things. A common metaphor used is that "sensors see the trees, while intuitives see the forest." If a sensor and an intuitive both walked through the forest, the sensor would be able to appreciate each tree on an individual level, while the intuitive would be too busy marveling at the totality of the forest. While sensors tend to live in the here and now, intuitives are more likely to think about the future.

Sensors tend to be down-to-earth and practical, while intuitives are creative and intrigued by the unknown. It would make sense then that sensors are the ones to get things done, while intuitives are the ones to dream things up. If you were to survey people that work with numbers or worked with their hands, odds are a good portion of them would be sensors. Take a poll of painters and writers, and you are much more likely to find intuitives.

Before you attempt to read someone's body language to tell if they are a sensor or an intuitive, here is some quick math: two out of every three people in the United States are sensors. This leaves one in three that are intuitives. Right off the bat, you have a 65% chance that the person you are trying to read is a sensor.

The body language differences between a sensor and an intuitive are not always clear. The biggest distinction is that sensors are usually more aware of their bodies. Sensors are known to have natural body movement, which is often perceived as athletic and graceful. Intuitives are known to be unaware of their body language and their surroundings. Awkward body language might be subjective, but it is a fairly accurate description of an intuitive's demeanors. Intuitives are much more likely to stub their toe or trip because they were not paying attention to their environment.

Thinking (T) vs. Feeling (F)

On the surface, it might be hard to determine which side of this spectrum you might fall on. Everyone has thoughts and feelings on a wide variety of subjects. When we make decisions and come to conclusions, we tend to favor either our thoughts or our feelings. Thinkers will look at a decision they need to make and use logic and reason to come to a final decision. Feelers can look at the exact same decision and consider what their values tell them is the right thing to do.

Thinkers often have analytical minds that can be incredibly useful for problem-solving, while feelers are high in empathy. Fields such as engineering and business are frequently dominated by thinkers who can objectively look at a problem and come up with the best way to solve it. Medical and teaching professions tend to be more dominated by feelers, who take great satisfaction in helping others.

A quick hack you can use if you are attempting to identify a thinker vs. a feeler is that two-thirds of men are known to be thinkers, while two-thirds of women are known to be feelers. While it might be tempting to always play the numbers, you should use caution. Don't assume all men are thinkers and all women feelers. It is a common stereotype of men to be aggressive and logical, while women are emotional and cooperative, but of course, this is not always the case.

A typical attribute of thinkers is that they may often come off as cooler, while feelers might come off as warmer. Feelers are often friendly to people they don't know. If your first impression of someone is "that person was nice," they are likely a feeler. While thinkers can be very polite, they often come off as more reserved because they do not care as much what you think of them. While feelers will be open and honest with you about their feelings, thinkers will hold their cards close to their chest. Another trait of feelers is that they are quick to give compliments, while thinkers are not.

When attempting to spot a feeler or a thinker, the best place to look is the face. Feelers will often show you many different facial expressions and are not shy about showing their feelings on their face. When they are excited, they smile, and when they are frightened, they are quick to show discomfort on their face. A telltale sign of a feeler is that they might have lines on their face around their eyes and mouth due to their many years of facial expressions.

Thinkers' facial expressions and body language are much harder to read than feelers, as they are less likely to openly display their emotions. One oddly specific body language cue that thinkers often utilize is counting out their thoughts. A thinker will count out the reasons why they believe something, even going so far as to count off their reasons on their fingers.

Judging (J) vs. Perceiving (P)

The final dimension is a tad bit deceptive in its wording. Judgers are not necessarily judgmental, and perceivers are not always very perceptive. The two ends of the spectrum are more related to openness. Judgers are more likely to form an opinion and stick to it, while perceivers are more likely to keep an open mind and accept new information. While judgers are much more decisive and at times stubborn, perceivers are often open-minded and at times indecisive.

A great way to look at judgers and perceivers is based on how they handle tension. A judger will likely feel tension when they are faced with a decision, and thus they will feel the need to make that decision as soon as possible. Likewise, a perceiver feels tension by being forced to make a decision and will thus delay having to decide for as long as possible. If you are someone that often jumps the gun and makes snap decisions on an impulse, you are a judger. If you are someone that likes to procrastinate and delay the inevitable, you are a perceiver.

Judgers represent 60% of the population, while perceivers represent 40%. Judgers are known to carry themselves with formal or serious demeanors, even to the point where they literally appear to be weighed down by their conventionalism. Oppositely, perceivers are less formal and are light on their feet. Perceivers are often unconventional and irreverent; they don't take things as seriously as judgers.

The biggest giveaway on whether someone is a judger or a perceiver is their decisiveness. The next time you go out to a restaurant with someone that you do not know that well, take a moment to analyze how they order from the menu. Judgers are likely to pick a menu item and get it over with, while perceivers are likely to peruse and take their time. A perceiver might even reconsider their order once they have made it; something you will rarely see a judger do.

Outside of body language, speech can be a huge indicator for judgers. Judgers will use definitive words such as "absolutely" and "definitely," to indicate that there is no doubt in their mind. On the other hand, perceivers prefer to clarify their statements or make them open-ended. "As far as I can tell…" is something that you might hear a perceiver say before they say something of importance. They might also favor slang words such as "nah" or "yup," to more definitive words such as "no" and "yes."

The Four Temperaments

Now that we have established the four dimensions on which your personality can fall, we can examine individual personalities more closely. Were you able to determine your personality based on the four dimensions? If you haven't yet, give it a try. Take a quick second and determine where you fall on each dimension. The four traits that you landed on make up your individual personality.

We will delve deeper into the sixteen different personality types in Chapter 7. For now, let's break down the sixteen personality types into the temperament categories they fall into. Here is a useful chart that you can reference to keep track of the sixteen personalities and four temperaments:

Category	Personality Types	Temperament
Sensing Judgers	ESTJ, ISTJ, ESFJ, ISFJ	Traditionalists
Sensing Perceivers	ESTP, ISTP, ESFP, ISFP	Experiencers
Intuitive Thinkers	ENTJ, INTJ, ENTP, INTP	Conceptualizers
Intuitive Feelers	ENFJ, INFJ, ENFP, INFP	Idealists

If you were able to accurately pinpoint your personality type, you can also find your temperament. In general, most people fall into one of four temperaments: traditionalists, experiencers, conceptualizers, and idealists. Does one of the below temperament definitions describe you?

Traditionalists make up 40% of the American population. They value responsibility and service to society. They are organized people who need structure within their lives. Because they are reliable, dependable, and hardworking, you will often find traditionalists in positions of management. Traditionalists also see the importance of authority and power structures. They are also cautious people by nature. They set realistic goals for themselves and enjoy learning from experience.

Experiencers make up 30% of the American population. They are the most free-spirited of the four temperaments. Experiencers love spontaneity; taking life one day at a time as opposed to planning it all out. They enjoy physical stimulation and play, making them excellent athletes and performers. Because experiencers rarely worry about their future, they are much better short-term problem solvers. Experiencers are often referred to as fun-loving, risk-taking, or adventure-seeking.

Conceptualizers are much less common and make up 15% of the population. Conceptualizers like to think of things in terms of the big picture, and their focus is often on the future. Conceptualizers enjoy mental stimulation, and they use logic and objectivity to come to decisions. They can often be perfectionists that set very high standards for themselves and others. People that are conceptualizers have the ability to consider abstract ideas and theories, while at the same time be able to think objectively and analytically about a topic. Fiercely independent and skeptical by nature, conceptualizers are on a constant quest for knowledge.

Idealists make up the final 15% of the population. The most empathetic of the four temperaments, idealists are on a life-long journey of self-discovery. They make decisions based on emotions and their impact on other people. Idealists place high importance on maintaining strong values and integrity. Idealists are very perceptive of other people's feelings, which can help them be charismatic communicators. Known to possess the "soul of an artist," idealists are often original and creative thinkers.

Which one of these temperaments best describes you? Being able to understand yourself and your personality is the first step to understanding others.

If you're confident you've identified your personality type, you can easily go online and find out more about your personality type. You will likely be shocked at the accuracy of the personality profile. It may seem that the personality profile knows you better than your closest friends and family do! Don't be so sure, though. Let's try another little experiment. Instead of identifying your own personality type, pick someone you know extremely well. Use the four personality dimensions to identify their personality. Now see if your friend or relative agrees with your diagnosis. You might be surprised at how easy it is to identify the personality of someone you know well.

Once you have diagnosed the personalities of the people closest to you, the next logical step is diagnosing strangers. Although you don't need to memorize the sixteen personality types to speed-read people, being able to identify personality traits can be a huge asset for reading body language. In Chapter 6, we will revisit personality types and the specific tools you can use to identify personalities and speed-read them.

The Myers-Briggs test, while not perfect, is a valuable tool for understanding people. While we are all unique in our own way, we all share certain similarities that make us alike. Just as emotional intelligence is an excellent skill for building connections with people, understanding personalities can help bridge the gap between people that think differently than we do.

Visual Intelligence

Observation & Perception

The skills of observation and perception are essential to anyone wishing to become an effective reader of body language. There's just one problem: we live in an age of distraction. Every day our brains are being training to avoid boredom at all costs. We unconsciously reach for our phones instead of taking in our surroundings. The average American checks their phone roughly one hundred times a day. While your cellphone is an incredible invention that allows you to become connected to more humans than ever before, it also distracts you from the things right in front of your eyes. How many times have you seen a couple at a restaurant who are both on their phones instead of enjoying each other's company?

Seeing something is not necessarily observing. Sherlock Holmes, one of the most famous figures in the history of literature, solved seemingly impossible cases simply through the power of observation. He often could size people up with one glance. He could tell if someone was a habitual smoker by the tint of their teeth or determine if someone was a manual laborer by the calluses on their hands. In one of the Sherlock Holmes short stories written by Arthur Conan Doyle, Holmes gets into an argument with his assistant Dr. Watson, because Watson claims he has eyes equally as strong as Sherlock's. When Sherlock asks Watson how many stairs are in his home, Watson has no clue. Of course, Holmes knows there to be 17 steps. "You have not observed. And yet you have seen," Holmes tells Dr. Watson.

The art of observation involves attention to detail. We often go about our lives in such a hurried fashion that we never take the time to fully observe our surroundings. Distraction is the true enemy of observation. When our minds are focused on other tasks, we are unable to process all of the visual information that is being fed to our brains. If you've ever tried reading a book while your mind was elsewhere, you've most likely experienced this phenomenon. You might read a whole page of text, but only after you have read it will you realize that you comprehended none of it.

Humans are constantly being exposed to external stimuli. Our five senses are constantly filtering through the external stimuli that they are presented. Additionally, internal stimuli such as thoughts, daydreams, and memories are also battling for our attention. It would be impossible for our brain to consciously process all of the stimuli that is presented in any given second. The decision our brain makes to focus on one stimulus over the many others is known as attention. Without the ability to focus your attention, your brain would melt down due to overstimulation. Yet, attention has its flaws.

Perhaps you have seen the famous selective attention test created by Harvard psychologists Daniel Simons and Christopher Chabris in 1999. The video experiment depicts two teams of basketball players quickly passing around a basketball. The experiment asks the subject to count the number of passes the team in white makes. As the two teams pass around basketballs, a man in a gorilla costume walks into the middle of the frame, thumps his chest, and walks offscreen. Incredibly, 50% of test subjects did not notice the gorilla. Simons and Chabris referred to this phenomenon as "inattentional blindness."

We are constantly making conscious and unconscious decisions about what we want to pay attention to. Our brains are hardwired to take the path of least resistance, which means once we decide on what to pay attention to, everything else will become background noise. However, much like emotional intelligence, you can train yourself to improve visual intelligence. Like any other skill, you must first consciously and forcefully practice it, but after enough practice, it will become second nature. Neuroscientists agree with this point. The practice of new skills changes our brains' internal connections; in other words, it changes our brains' hardwiring.

To successfully read people, you must hone your perception skills. Oftentimes body language can be incredibly subtle and nuanced. To a typical observer, a slight head twitch from a colleague might mean nothing, but to the skilled observer that has mastered the art of perception, that head twitch tells quite an interesting story.

Learning Perception Through Art

Amy E. Herman is an art historian and lawyer who developed an educational course called *The Art of Perception*. Students of Herman's course include the NYPD, the FBI, Department of Homeland Security, the Secret Service, and the Department of Justice, to name a few. What does a class that teaches perception to the upper echelons of law enforcement entail? Herman has her students look at art. She discovered that through the analysis of art, her students could greatly improve their observation skills. This suggests that skills such as observation and perception can be developed alone. You do not need to practice your observation skills on someone else. You can practice with a painting.

The first thing to know before you begin to bolster your visual intelligence is that all of the information you perceive is edited through your subconscious filter. This point is best exemplified in the world of art. Art is completely perception-based. No two people will look at the same painting and have the same impression of it. Think of your favorite movies, books, and songs. Do you know anyone that shares your opinions on art completely? Of course not. We all have our own subconscious filters that are made up of our personal experiences and preferences.

An excellent example of the concept of subconscious filters is Tony Matelli's 2014 sculpture, *Sleepwalker*. Installed on campus at Wellesley College, the realistic sculpture of a middle-aged man in his underwear with his arms outstretched and his eyes closed upset many people. Many mistook the sculpture for a real man. Many were terribly frightened by what they thought resembled a drug addict or a threatening attacker. Others found the sculpture humorous and took selfies with it. Depending on the subconscious filters of those who viewed Matelli's sculpture, there was a wide variety of feelings toward it. As is also typical with art, the more polarizing the piece, the wider the difference of opinion will be.

It is incredibly difficult, if not impossible, to remove your subconscious filter. The moment you perceive something, your brain categorizes the new information based on the way you have trained it to perceive information. The list of things that could be influencing your subconscious filter are endless, but some include past experiences, geographic history, values, culture, religion, political affiliations, education, upbringing, taste, desires, finances, mood, physical state, groups you belong to, and prior information. Next time you are using perception on a piece of information someone has revealed to you, don't rush to judgment. Take a moment and think about which of your subconscious filters might be influencing your perception of this new information. Will your initial perception remain intact?

Perhaps the most common subconscious filter has to do with confirmation bias. As we discussed in Chapter 2, confirmation bias is looking for pieces of information that confirm what we already believe and ignoring information that goes against our beliefs. In other words, seeing what we want to see. A team manager who believes that one individual on their team is holding everyone else back might begin to examine this team member's performance more scrupulously and evaluate it more harshly. A police officer who is convinced their suspect committed the crime will naturally be more perceptive of evidence that points to guilt than evidence that points to innocence.

The best way to avoid your subconscious filters is to stick to the facts. When you observe someone, be careful to distinguish your thoughts between provable facts and assumptions. If you see someone wearing a very expensive watch, you might assume that they are well-off and come from money. But perhaps the watch was a gift; they only wear it to overcompensate for the fact that they are living paycheck to paycheck. The provable fact in your observation is that they are wearing an expensive watch. You might even be able to identify the brand or price of the watch by looking at it. While it might feel like a safe bet that this person is well-off, you must remember to categorize this thought as an assumption until you can confirm it as fact. As you compile more facts, they will point you closer to a factual assumption.

When you are attempting to speed-read someone, you must be extremely attentive and pay attention to the little details. You also must be able to think critically about who the person is that you are speed-reading. The best way to do this is to ask yourself four simple questions: who, what, when, and where?

Let's play out another hypothetical scenario to test our four questions of perception. You are riding on a subway train in New York City on a Monday morning. You spot a man standing across from you and you decide you will practice your developing speed-reading skills on him. Start with the four questions.

Who? While you might not be able to deduce the man's name from looking at him, you can still begin to build a profile. He is dressed in a suit and tie. He holds a briefcase. Based on the quality of his suit you assume that whatever his job is, it pays well. Maybe he works on Wall Street. But again, this is an assumption; we'll stick to facts. He is not sporting a wedding ring, which means either he is not yet a family man, or he is divorced. If he has a job working in a highly competitive job market like New York City, he likely has a college degree. This would make him older than 21. He has a thick head of jet-black hair and no wrinkles on his face. The common laws of nature would indicate that he is likely younger than 40.

What? Is there anything about the way this man is acting that might give you clues as to who he is? He is clutching his suitcase close to his chest, almost giving it a bear hug. He appears protective over the case. Is he carrying something valuable? Or is he new to the subway system and overcautious of theft? His knee is jumping up and down with a case of restless leg syndrome. Clearly, this young man is anxious about something. Perhaps an upcoming job interview or presentation at the office?

When? It is a Monday morning, so it is natural to see commuters on the subway at this time. But let's be more specific. It's 6 AM on the last Monday of September. 6 AM is a little early to get to the office. Perhaps this young man is the first one in the office every morning. Or perhaps he is playing it safe and making sure he has plenty of time to find the building and be on time for his job interview. This is an assumption, but right now more facts are pointed toward this assumption. September is also a common time of year for companies to bring on board a fresh batch of college graduates. If this is not a job interview, perhaps it is his first day at a new job.

Where? The New York City Subway. But can we get any more specific? How about the stop in which the young man gets off? You wait patiently, and sure enough, the young man gets off the train at the Wall Street station. It would certainly seem that this young man is a mid-20s college grad that is beginning (or trying to begin) his Wall Street career. Is this an assumption? Yes, but the facts back you up. If you are playing the odds, fact-based assumptions are often the best chances you have of accurately reading your mark.

The nervous young man on the subway may not be a difficult person to read, but it shows how our mind works when we read people. You might take one look at that young man, and without thinking, deduce he is on his way to a job interview. You might not even consciously note all the detail of the who, what, when, and where. Our subconscious mind has been trained in convenient shortcuts to judgments, which can often be accurate. However, to become a great reader of people, you must learn to contextualize the shortcuts. Understand the details and visuals that lead you to make judgments. Soon you will be able to catch yourself before you make a false assumption or take a closer look and notice a previously unforeseen detail.

Another useful trick to add to your perception toolbox is information prioritization. When we read a person or situation, our brains are taking in a lot of information at once. Information prioritization is the idea that all of the information that our brain takes in is not created equal. In almost all scenarios, there are pieces of information that are more important than others. Law enforcement officers use information prioritization all of the time. When they are interviewing a suspect or investigating a crime scene, there will be certain information that is irrelevant, and other information that is pivotal to cracking a case.

Amy E. Herman has a great example of how information prioritization can often be overlooked. In one of her classes, she paired people up into partners. One partner was allowed to look at a picture and recite what they saw, while the other partner had to write down what their partner told them. Over the course of a minute, half of the students recited details of the picture to their partners. The picture showed a pumpkin patch with many smashed pumpkins, and in the backdrop, a house was on fire. By the end of the minute,

Herman found that many of the students did not even mention the burning house to the partner. The students claimed that they had seen the burning house, but they didn't have the time to relay that information to their partner in under a minute. This class consisted of 911 operators.

This anecdote perfectly encapsulates the importance of information prioritization. If a burning house is not prioritized over the details of a pumpkin patch, you should consider prioritizing your information in different ways.

Joel Sternfeld, McLean, Virginia, December 1978.

One of the most well-established ways of prioritizing information comes from Richards J. Heuer's *Psychology of Intelligence Analysis.* Heuer uses three main questions to help prioritize. What do I know, what don't I know, and if I could get more information, what do I need to know?

Let's use the above photograph and apply Heuer's strategy of information prioritization. What do I know from looking at this photograph? We can see that there is a farm market with many crushed pumpkins. There appears to be someone standing in front of the farm market, though it is not clear if it is a man or a woman. In the background, we can see a house that is on fire. The fire department is on the scene of the fire and is attempting to put it out. There are other more specific details in the photo, but we'll stick to those for now. How should we prioritize this information? It depends. If we're using danger as the metric of prioritization, the burning house is easily the most important thing in the picture. But now imagine that you are a police officer investigating the property damage of the farm market's pumpkins. If this was the case, the person standing in front of the pumpkin patch might become the most important piece of information. If they are not the owner of the establishment, they may be a suspect.

The most important part of information prioritization is having a goal in mind when you prioritize. What are you hoping to accomplish by reading the situation or person? When you know what your endgame is, you can better pick out the most relevant pieces of information that will help you.

So, what don't we know from looking at the above photo? We don't know how the fire started or how the pumpkins got smashed. Is it possible the two are related? Is there foul play involved? Oftentimes the best way to examine the question of what I don't know is to look for information that is missing. Don't look at what is in the photo, look for what isn't. Do you notice anything missing? How about leaves on the trees? It would certainly appear to be fall or winter by the looks of the naked trees. Perhaps the fire was accidental and caused by someone trying to start a fire for warmth. Notice anything else missing? Metal vertical bars are sticking out of the ground that appear to be for some sort of fencing, but there is no fence surrounding the market. This might have given critters and scavengers free rein of the pumpkin patch.

Finally, if we could get more information, what do we need to know? The important unanswered information is this: who is standing in front of the farm market, what happened to the pumpkins, and how did the fire start? If we had to prioritize one of these unknowns, which would it be? Most would probably say how did the fire start. The fire is the most pertinent element of the photo, and there is no indication that the person at the market and the pumpkins have anything to do with the fire.

We can eliminate one right off the bat. Nothing happened to the pumpkins. At least, nothing unnatural. The pumpkins that rotted and became unsellable were simply left out in the field. Any foul play or intent to destroy the pumpkins was an assumption, and in this case, the assumption was incorrect.

Next, who is the person in front of the market? The answer to this question will change your view of the photograph completely. The person in front of the market is a fireman, apparently shopping for pumpkins while a house burns behind him. This is quite a striking image and one that leads the viewer to jump to all sorts of conclusions. We can assume that the fireman is acting in negligence because he is shopping for pumpkins instead of doing his duty and putting out a blazing fire.

Finally, how did the fire start? Again, the answer to this question will change your perception of the photograph, and finally, allow us to understand what we are looking at. The fire was a training exercise conducted by the fire department. The fireman at the farm market was simply perusing pumpkins while he was on his break.

Prioritizing the information about the fire would prove to give us a clear understanding of what actually occurred in this picture. The broken pumpkins turned out to be unimportant to the overall situation. The identity of the individual in the picture completely changed our understanding of the picture, but if we were to have prioritized the person's identity over the cause of the fire, it would have given us an incomplete and misleading view of reality. The cause of the fire was the top priority question in this situation, and it proved to be the main story behind the photo.

If your goal in reading this book is to become a master speed reader, then the tools of observation and perception will take you far. Try practicing on art before you practice on people. If you can, go to an art museum and view paintings you have never seen before. If you don't have access to an art museum, go online and view some famous art. Take a full minute and observe the painting. Mentally note everything you can about the painting. Be as specific as possible. Now take a half-hour and forget about the painting. After that half-hour, how much can you remember? Could you draw a rough sketch from memory?

Perception and observation are two tools that can easily be sharpened with practice. If you are committed and you continue to practice, you will notice results. You will begin to notice things that others don't. You will become more observant, more detail-oriented, and a better judge of people.

Take care when you practice perception. Avoid the pitfalls and traps that come with it. Like in the photo of the burning house, oftentimes things are not as they seem. You can be incredibly perceptive, but if you perceive information that is intended to deceive you, you can still walk away with an inaccurate understanding of people. There is only one way to avoid this trap. You must be able to recognize the tricks and habits that reveal phonies. In the next chapter, we will discuss how you can avoid being duped. You will learn how to spot a liar.

Spotting a Liar

They're Everywhere

It is not hyperbole to say that everybody lies. The average person lies 1.65 times a day. Just because we all lie, does not make us inherently evil. We lie for many reasons, some better than others. We might lie to protect someone's feelings. We lie to save face and avoid embarrassment. We lie because we are scared of being judged. We lie to deliberately deceive. We even lie because we feel like it. Sometimes stretching the truth, or adding an untrue element, can turn a boring story into a great one.

We tend to think of lies as a calculated act of deceit, which can sometimes be the case, but they are often more complicated than that. Lies are rooted in emotion. As we have established in earlier chapters, emotion often can lead to a mistake in judgment. Studies have shown that we are better at spotting liars when they are complete strangers than when they are someone close to us. When our emotions are clouded with our prior emotions for individuals, we can be blind to the truth.

There are three ways in which people lie. The first is a complete lie. This is a fabrication, pure and simple. The second is a mix of the truth and a lie. Mixing a lie in with the undeniable truth will make any lie go down smoother. Finally, there is lying by omission. Telling the truth is always easier than lying because you don't have to make anything up or keep your stories straight. Many people also believe that omitting the truth is not directly lying because nothing untrue has been said. However, when the omission of truth is damning enough to completely change someone's perception, that is as good as a lie.

As your skills as a speed reader progress and you can spot lies more and more readily, you must remember to take one thing to heart: don't take a lie personally. The more emotion you bring into the equation, the less effective you will be as a speed reader. Don't let your ego get in the way of your objective analysis of someone. People are complex creatures, and they lie for a myriad of reasons. When people lie, they rarely do it as a personal affront to someone else. They are thinking about their own self-interests or worried about their ego.

Before we go into specific body language that gives away liars, let's discuss the one foolproof strategy that anyone can use to spot a liar. It is the preferred method of spotting liars that is used by FBI interrogators, polygraph examiners, and criminal profilers. The strategy is this: be an active listener. While this might not be the sexy answer you were hoping for, think about it. What could be a better strategy for reading someone than active listening? Let your mind do the reading, while the other person reveals all.

Next time you are in a conversation with someone, put your ego to the side and allow them to dominate the conversation. Do not sit there and think about what you are going to say next, but instead listen and analyze what they are saying. You can ask them primer questions to keep them talking. People love to talk about themselves. So, ask them a question about themselves and let them start talking. As we discussed in the previous chapter, the key to perception is not just noticing the information that is available but noticing the information that has been withheld. If someone is telling you a story about themselves, why did they choose to pick that specific story? Why did they embellish one part of the story with very specific details, and in other parts of the story the details were vague and uneven? Does the story seem rehearsed or spontaneous? In general, vague details and a rehearsed quality are both warning signs for lies.

To spot a liar you don't have to do much work at all. Just remain vigilant, pay attention to the little details of the conversation, and let the other person do most of the talking. It is a common misconception that the person who does all the talking controls the conversation. Really, it is the opposite. Those who know how to listen can push the conversation in a direction without the talker noticing. All the while, the active listener is collecting intel and waiting to spot the lie.

The Tells of a Liar – Body Language

Have you ever had a conversation with someone and suspected that they might be lying? What was it that made you suspect the person was being untruthful? You might not have been able to put it into words. Call it a sixth sense. Whatever the case, your instincts are often much better than you may suspect. Our brain subconsciously picks up on speech patterns and body language much more efficiently than our conscious brain. If you get a bad feeling about someone you just met, there is likely a good reason, even if you can't pinpoint it. In this section, we will work on developing how to take your subconscious judgments of people and elevate them to the conscious level.

Just as everyone lies, everyone has tells. A tell is something a person will inadvertently do that will reveal that they are lying. Most commonly tells come in the form of body language, demeanor, or attitude. It can also be verbal; for instance, someone who nervously talks a lot when they are hiding something. The concept of a tell is often associated with poker, where players will bluff and bet big when they have poor hands. Being able to spot a tell at a poker table can be a very lucrative skill. When poker players look for tells, they are not looking for universal signs that someone is lying. They study someone's behavior and mannerisms, and they watch for patterns. Tells, as poker players know, are different for everyone.

Unfortunately, there are no universal tells that can expose liars. Every individual is unique. Everyone talks differently, acts differently, and lies differently. However, there is some good news. Most people are poor liars. Lying requires a vivid memory to recall the stories you are fabricating (and separate them from the truth). Lying also requires extreme self-awareness; the ability to project confidence and sell their story without appearing dishonest. Accomplishing these two things at once is a high-wire act that more than not leads to mistakes. Liars also rarely know their tells. They are unwittingly exposed. All it takes is a person practiced in the art of perception to spot their lie.

Body language is the key to spotting liars. As was discussed at the beginning of the book, 55% of communication is nonverbal. The quickest way to spot a liar is to watch for body language that does not agree with their speech. Incongruence between speech and body language is something that we will pick up subconsciously; it is second nature to us. If someone says they are open to an idea, but their arms are crossed and they're avoiding eye contact, they are just telling you what you want to hear. If someone tells you they are having a great time at a party, but they've been sitting in the corner staring at their hands, you won't believe what they are telling you.

A disconnect between speech and body language can often be so obvious it is astounding. People have been known to reveal their lies to "yes or no" questions by their head movements. If someone responds "yes" to a question and subtly moves their head side-to-side, their body language is revealing the truth while their speech is lying. On a subconscious level, most humans understand that lying is wrong. This is why our bodies will rebel against a spoken lie and seek to reveal the truth.

Again, not all lies are evil and manipulative. Some are innocuous and used as a shield. When couples and spouses go through rough patches, it is often due to a lack of communication. One-half of the couple might repeatedly say "I'm fine," when asked what is wrong. Being able to spot body language that doesn't line up with speech can help any couple that is struggling in their relationship. Oftentimes we lie because we are scared to vocalize our feelings. Other times we lie because we want to spare someone the burden of having to listen to our feelings.

Spotting body language that doesn't agree with speech is much easier to do with people we know. The more we grow to know someone, the more we recognize their patterns of behavior. This begs the question: how do we spot incongruent patterns in people that we have only just met? The simple answer is that you must get to know them. Getting to know someone does not mean learning their life story. You can learn a lot about a person by having one conversation with them. Specifically, you can discover their baseline.

Finding a person's baseline is a strategy used by criminal interrogators and law enforcement all over the country. It is a concept that we will use throughout this chapter. A person's baseline is their normal behavior and body language. In this case, "normal" can be defined as when the person has nothing to hide.

When an interrogator interviews a suspect, they do not open up the conversation by asking if the suspect is guilty. This would immediately put them on guard. They start with easy questions. Questions that will put the subject at ease. Where are you from? Do you have any kids? I like that shirt, where'd you get it? These questions are not meant to extract juicy pieces of information. These questions are used to see how someone behaves when they have their guard down. Interrogators watch their suspects and mentally note each mannerism that occurs when they are causally conversing. Once they have a general idea of a subject's baseline, they can move forward with the stress-inducing questions. If a question is asked that causes body language well outside a person's baseline, the interrogator will mentally make note of the red flag. The interrogator now knows what line of questioning needs to be explored further.

Just because someone's body language gives off a red flag does not mean they are lying. Sometimes natural body language just happens to time itself out so that it appears like a lie. Other times there might be more to the story than a simple yes or no answer.

A woman asks her boyfriend if he got dinner with his father last night, and the boyfriend responds yes, but he looks to the floor when he speaks. This girlfriend immediately recognizes the body language in her boyfriend as a red flag. She fears the worst. Is he cheating on her? In reality, the boyfriend is not lying about getting dinner with his father. What the boyfriend is hiding is that after dinner his father helped him pick out an engagement ring at a jewelry store. In this situation, the red flag was an indication that there was more to the story than a simple yes or no, but the boyfriend was not lying about getting dinner with his father.

The pitfalls of assumptions that we discussed in the previous chapter can be equally perilous when spotting liars. Red flags can lead us to the truth, but they will never come out and explicitly tell us what the truth is. This is why it is important to look for clusters of behavior as opposed to one specific piece of body language. The more information you gather, the better equipped you are to develop your assumption into a well-supported observation. The more red flags you spot, the more confident you will become that the person speaking to you is lying through their teeth.

Spotting liars is not a science. The best we can do is observe, note everything we see, identify behavior outside of the baseline (red flag), and examine that particular behavior further. There are a few common areas where red flags in body language can appear. While one red flag is never enough to indict someone for lying, a cluster of red flags could be damning evidence.

Eyes

Contrary to popular opinion, if someone maintains eye contact with you, that does not mean that they are telling the truth. If someone is a skilled liar, they might purposefully hold eye contact with you while they lie to your face. Baseline eye contact will be the benchmark when spotting red flags. When a person speaks casually to you about the weather, how often do they hold eye contact? Statistically, people only hold eye contact for 60% of conversations. Some people naturally hold more eye contact, and others hold less. A person's baseline level of eye contact might be no eye contact at all. Whatever the baseline level of eye contact is, observe it, and watch for discrepancies.

One of the most common mistakes made by people is to instruct a liar on how to behave. We see this often in mothers disciplining their children or spouses trying to pry the truth from their partner. "I want you to look into my eyes and tell me the truth," are famous last words. People believe that by looking into someone's eyes, they will be able to decipher the truth. In reality, when you say those words to someone, you are training them how to behave when they lie to you. If a young child is told by their mother to look into mommy's eyes and tell the truth, the child will eventually learn to look into mommy's eyes when he is lying to her. Do not throw liars lifelines by telling them how to act or behave. Observe their behavior that occurs naturally. Eventually, the red flags will reveal themselves.

Another trick used by interrogators is to ask a suspect a basic recall question. It is common for people to look upward when they are recalling information. For example, if you ask someone what was their favorite birthday present that they ever received, they might look up and to the left, as if they are literally searching their brain for the answer. Now ask the same person a more personal question that requires recall. How many times have you been arrested? Where do their eyes go this time? Going off their established baseline, a look up and to the left would be an honest recall, while a look down indicates they are hiding something.

One common eye expression is the upward eye roll. This is a universal symbol of exasperation. A person rolling their eyes at you might lead you to believe they are annoyed with you, and you might be right. However, an upward eye roll means something more specific. It indicates that the person does not wish to talk about the current topic of discussion. While this is not necessarily a red flag, it can be a good indicator that the current line of conversation is a trigger for the person. The person likely has thoughts on the topic that they do not wish to vocalize.

Another common eye expression is the deer in headlights. This usually entails a frozen stare of fear. If someone is a poor liar, they may immediately revert to a deer in headlights look when they are caught in a lie. This look is powered by fear, which is an extremely powerful emotion. Most people are unqualified to control their fear, which makes fear a great catalyst for exposing liars. When fear takes over, a person can lose control of their facial and body expressions completely. Hence, the deer in headlights look.

One final red flag that you may spot in someone's eyes is seeing the whites of their eyes. Observe someone's eyes in their natural state. You will see their iris and the whites of their eyes to the right and left of the iris. A person's eyes will often widen when they are in a state of shock. If you can see the whites of someone's eyes above or below their iris, this should be a red flag to you. This eye expression might be so brief that it lasts for little more than a second. Now you know why professional poker players wear sunglasses.

Mouth

Mouths are where lies originate from. Oftentimes young children will cover their mouths when they tell a lie. It's as if they are subconsciously trying to catch the lie before it escapes their mouth. Watching someone's mouth when they speak could very well reveal what they really think about what they are saying. A clenched jaw or grinding teeth can often indicate anger in someone. Biting down on lips or curling lips to one side might also be a sign that someone is subconsciously uncomfortable with what they are saying.

When someone is nervous, they often get a dry mouth. How many times in the movies have we seen a nervous suspect in the interrogation room swallow repeatedly or gulp down a glass of water to calm their nerves? This is an exaggerated, but not inaccurate portrayal of dry-mouth nervousness. Of course, someone could be nervous because they feel they are being threatened, which would not indicate they are lying.

Oddly enough, studies have shown that yawning is another common expression of liars. Like the dry mouth, yawning is a natural reaction of the body to calm someone's nerves. The more stress someone is put under, the more likely they will yawn. A deep gulp of oxygen to the body can quite literally help cool off someone's nerves. While dry mouth and yawning are common signs of stress that occur during interrogations, these are unlikely red flags to appear in casual conversation.

When watching a suspected liar's mouth, beware of their smiles. A manipulative liar will use a smile to try and disarm you, but it is rarely genuine. Studies have shown that the way to tell a real smile from a phony one is to look at someone's eyes. A genuine smile will completely change someone's face. A smile will raise the corners of your cheeks and mouth, will cause the eyes to squint, and can last up to four seconds. A fake smile will only transform the bottom half of your face. If you look in someone's eyes when they shoot you a fake smile, you will notice that there is no change in the top half of their face. A fake smile can be used out of nervousness or politeness. It could also be used out of disingenuous manipulation. Always watch the eyes when someone shoots you a smile.

The mouth can also work to subconsciously release tension with laughter. Laugher is often out of a person's control. When someone is asked a stressful question, it might be their natural reaction to laugh. They don't necessarily find the question humorous, but laughter is a way for them to immediately release their tension at that moment. If someone laughs during an unusual part of a conversation, make a mental note of it. Why did they feel the need to release tension at this particular moment?

Upper Body

Let's start with the hands. Hands are one of the best tools we have for communicating nonverbally. Studies have shown that people who gesture with their hands when they are talking appear more confident. This is why it is natural for a liar to try and hide their hands. A liar is often operating under the fear that they are going to be found out. They fear their hands could reveal something that they want to remain hidden, and thus they will move their hands out of sight. A person who puts their hands in their pockets, sits on their hands, or tucks their hands away might be hiding something.

A skilled liar might leave their hands in plain sight but still refrain from hand gestures. If someone's baseline behavior includes illustrious hand gestures and body language, watch for whenever their hands go rigid and still. A spontaneous story from a person like this would be filled with over-the-top and confident hand gestures. A rehearsed story would more likely include still hands. A liar often rehearses their story, but not their performance.

Fidgeting is another obvious tell that can expose a liar. Fidgeting is a common reaction to nervousness and anxiety. Someone might appear restless or unable to sit still. They might bite their fingernails, shake their knees, or scratch themselves. Keep an open eye for restless body language when a difficult question is asked of someone. Conversely, if someone is a naturally restless and anxious person, watch out for them to flick a switch into a cool and calm demeanor when a tough question is asked. When you are looking for a lie, never forget to always consider body language in relation to the person's baseline.

Similar to fidgeting is the behavior of grooming. A woman twirling her hair or a man pulling on his beard might be a sign of deceit. Oftentimes liars might pretend to straighten their clothes or pick imaginary lint. Grooming is a common way for someone to avoid immediately addressing your question head-on. While a liar may think that a distracted appearance makes them appear nonchalant, really what they are doing is releasing their nervous energy.

You should also be cognizant of posture when you are attempting to read someone. Posture is a great indicator of mood. Whether a person's baseline posture is slouching or upright, make a mental note. Does the slouch indicate insecurity, guilt, or calmness? Does the upright posture reveal confidence, arrogance, or defiance? Watch for a freeze in someone's posture. A frozen posture brought on by fear might be a warning sign for an upcoming lie.

Lower Body

When attempting to spot a liar, a full view of the person is always preferable. If you are sitting across a table from someone, their face and upper body might be telling you one thing, while their lower body is telling another story entirely. Fidgeting legs, as was mentioned earlier, are an indicator of nervous energy. Similarly, crossed legs can reveal a closed-off or defensive state of mind.

Another key to lower body language is spacing between a person. If you are speaking with someone and they are keeping a safe distance, this might mean they are not invested in the conversation. Of course, this does not mean they are lying, but this is all dependent on the content of the conversation. Keep an eye out for a slight backpedal when someone is hit with a tough question. This subconscious backup is someone's body language revealing that they want no part of the conversation.

The Tells of a Liar – Speech

Tells are most often associated with body language because they are subconscious. Even the best liars have trouble hiding their body language. But not all liars operate on a subconscious level. Oftentimes liars can be defensive, disrespectful, or empathetic. There are many strategies that liars can use to cast doubt in people that question them. In this section, we will examine common speech patterns that liars may use to deceive you.

It is worth reiterating that if you encounter anyone who uses one of these phrases or speech patterns, that does not make them a liar. But perhaps these phrases only come out under stress, when this person is outside their baseline. Keep your ears open for any of these phrases, and mentally take note of them. If a common pattern of speech becomes apparent when someone is put under stress, you may be being deceived.

For the sake of brevity, we will use hypothetical husband (H) and wife (W) characters to illustrate how these strategies of lying are used. In our hypothetical scenario, the wife suspects the husband of infidelity and is questioning him. While this is an extreme scenario for spotting a liar, it works well as an example.

The first speech strategy a liar might use is to make you feel stupid for asking that question. This is a bullying tactic. The main goal of this strategy is to belittle the person and make them second guess their line of questioning. If someone is nervous about asking a question, a liar might attempt to turn their nervousness into submission. If you back off with your questioning, the liar will win. Here are some typical exchanges that might fall under this category:

W: Are you having an affair?
H1: That's a stupid question.
H2: You already asked me that.
H3: Do I have to answer that again?

A similar strategy is a dismissive response that lets you know that question is beneath you. This is a sneaky tactic because it shifts the blame toward the questioner. The liar is not in the wrong, but rather it is the questioner who has crossed the line for asking a question they already know the answer to.

W: Where were you Saturday night?
H1: I've already told you this; I was playing poker with the guys.
H2: As I assume you already know, I was playing poker with the guys.
H3: You know exactly where I was. I was playing poker with the guys.

Defensive liars will also make you feel guilty for wasting their time. A guilty liar will present themselves as above the line of questioning. The questions they are being asked are petty and silly, and not worth their precious time.

W: I feel as if you are lying to me. Can we talk about it?
H1: How long is this going to take?
H2: I don't have time for this.
H3: I have more important things to do.

Many liars are less aggressive with their tactics. They might be well aware that the person questioning them is not going to back down, or they might feel shame over their lies.

By refusing to commit to an answer, they feel as if they are being vague enough where they can avoid being caught.

>*W: Is there anything else you want to tell me about Saturday night?*
>
>*H1: I'm pretty sure I told you everything.*
>*H2: Nothing else comes to mind.*
>*H3: I don't think there's anything else to tell.*

Another classic move of the liar is to lie by omission. Rather than admit to anything, they will simply feign forgetfulness. This is also much easier than making up an elaborate lie.

>*W: Well, where were you when I called your office last month and they told me you weren't there?*
>*H1: I don't know.*
>*H2: I have no idea.*
>*H3: I forget.*

The non-answer is when a liar answers a different question than the one they were asked. While a liar knows that their answer doesn't directly answer the question, they are hoping it is enough to satisfy the questioner.

>*W: How about last Friday when your office told me you were getting lunch. Who were you getting lunch with?*
>*H1: I usually get lunch with my boss on Fridays.*
>*H2: I'm a busy man. I take out all kinds of clients to lunch.*
>*H3: I'm in sales. Going out to lunch is part of my job.*

The truth is simple, and the more bells and whistles attached to an answer, the more suspicious you should be. Oftentimes when someone is trying to sell you a lie, they will overreach. They will make all kinds of bold proclamations in order to convince you of their honesty. What they are really doing is overcompensating for their lie. We call this strategy the divine intervention.

> W: Why don't I believe you?
> H1: I swear to God I'm not cheating on you.
> H2: As God is my witness, I am not cheating on you.
> H3: I swear on my mother's grave that I am not cheating.

Liars often use common phrases known as integrity qualifiers. These are tacked onto an answer in an attempt to emphasize the honesty of their statement. It is possible that such integrity qualifiers are part of someone's baseline speech patterns, but if they are not, make sure not to miss them as a method for cloaking a lie.

> W: So, you're not cheating on me?
> H1: Honestly, I would never cheat on you.
> H2: In all truthfulness, I would never cheat on you.
> H3: To be perfectly honest with you, it never even crossed my mind.

This next red flag is not so much a strategy as it is a mistake that liars often make. It can be hard to catch, so make sure to listen carefully to the word choice of the suspected liar. Verb tenses can often reveal that someone is being disingenuous. The reason is simple: true stories live in the past, lies are made up in the present. If a person continually uses the present tense to tell a story that supposedly took place in the past, this is a giant red flag.

W: Why do you smell like someone else's perfume?

H1: So, I walk into this boutique shop looking for a gift for you...

H2: Billy in accounting asks me if I can smell this perfume he got his wife...

H3: I'm in line at the grocery store and this elderly woman stands in front of me...

Finally, one thing you might notice in a liar's speech is their removal of "I." "I" is one of the most commonly used words in the English language. When someone is talking about themselves, it is almost impossible to avoid using the word. A liar might remove this word from their statements because they are afraid to take ownership for their lies. It is a way to distance themselves from the falsehoods they are perpetrating.

W: Alright. Well, I guess I believe you.

H1: That's great. Love you.

H2: Okay good. Need to run to the store really quick. Be back soon.

H3: Great. Will be back home around 9:00 tonight.

When it comes to all of the above speech patterns, the only way you will catch them is by being an active listener. In the hypothetical situation we used, it is unlikely that the suspicious wife can be an objective and active listener to her husband's lies. Assuming she loves her husband, it would be almost impossible for her to avoid the influence of her emotions. To be a great reader of people, you must remember that all people will reveal themselves to you as long as you remain vigilant and objective.

Remember: everyone lies. A true objective speed reader will be able to identify lies, take note of them, but do not take offense. This chapter might even inspire you to think about how often you lie. Once you notice the surprising number of times you lie in a given week, you might be less judgmental when you catch someone in a lie. Also, a speed reader does not have time to take offense. If you are actively speed-reading and putting your skills to use in a conversation, you need to leave your emotions at the door.

Mastering Conversation

This chapter will be the last before we take the full plunge into the art of speed-reading and body language fluency. Before we take the deep dive, we need to talk about the art of the conversation.

Reading body language is an art with deep roots in empathy and understanding. In reading this book, you are searching for tools that will help you more effectively connect with people. It will all be for naught, however, if you cannot convince someone that you are worth the time to talk to. While active listening is a huge part of reading people, no one is looking for someone to sit silently while they blab on about themselves. That is called a psychiatrist. People open up to other people if they trust them, or if they want to win them over.

Let's say that you are reading this book to attract someone of the opposite sex. You've studied up on your emotional and visual intelligence, you have a decent understanding of human nature, and you are well versed in body language. So, with this newfound knowledge, you decide that the next time you are at a bar you are going to walk up to an attractive person of the opposite sex and start a conversation. There's just one problem: you don't know what to say. You would be able to quickly tell if the person is into you or not by their body language, but you're not sure how to be a naturally likable person. Sure, you could memorize some corny pickup lines, but how far will that get you?

This chapter is not about supplying you with content for conversation. That should occur naturally and be dependent on the person you are speaking to. Nor will this chapter be about tricking someone into liking you. This chapter is designed to give you proven strategies for being likable. Believe it or not, there are certain behaviors and attitudes that are universally well-received.

Conversation is the medium through which speed readers receive their messages. As a speed reader, adding conversation skills to your toolkit is never a bad idea. Of course, the conversation lives and dies by the first impression. A great first impression will leave a lasting impact on someone. On the other hand, a poor first impression may be impossible to overcome.

First Impressions

The average attention span for a human being is thirty seconds. This is not to say that humans are incapable of paying attention to something for longer than thirty seconds, but that we are by nature, impatient beings. If we become bored by something, we are quick to look for another form of mental stimulation. When you meet someone new, you should seek to make an immediate impact. Don't give them a reason to become bored and seek entertainment elsewhere.

The greeting comes first. The first thing someone will notice when you walk up to them is your body language. What do you think the ideal body language would be for a first impression? Open, of course. Open body language projects the idea that you are honest and forthright; that you have nothing to hide. Don't cross your arms. Don't put your hands in your pockets. If you are wearing a jacket or coat, leave it open. Keep your shoulders square and directly facing the person you are talking to. Open body language naturally reeks of confidence.

Your greeting should include direct eye contact. If the person you are approaching is not looking at you, initiate eye contact and allow them to meet your gaze. Imagine meeting someone new and they don't look you directly in the eyes. You would likely think to yourself: what are they hiding? Do they have a problem with me? Direct and steady eye contact also signals to the person you are talking to that your full attention is directed toward them.

The next part of the greeting is the smile. This is the hardest part of the greeting because as we've already covered, a perceptive person can spot a fake smile. It is also common for people to feel self-conscious about smiling at someone first. The key is to go in with a friendly and upbeat attitude. Don't carry expectations into the meeting. Ultimately, how the person reacts to you will be out of your control. A smile shows the person that you are sincere and friendly. Two important pieces of science show why smiling first can have such a positive impact on a first impression. First, studies show that people tend to mimic the facial expressions of people they talk to. Meaning a person is much more likely to smile at you if they see you smiling first. Second, smiling creates a natural release of dopamine, endorphins, and serotonin within the brain. These chemicals work to lower anxiety and increase happiness.

After the smile comes the verbal greeting. What you say is not all that important; whether it be "hello," "hi," or "how're you doing?" What is important is the tone in which you speak. Use a pleasant tonality. You want to appear enthusiastic about the conversation ahead, but don't appear overexcited. Don't shout. Keep eye contact and smile when you say hello. Also, be the first to introduce yourself. Say your name, and make sure you get the person's name when they introduce themselves. If you can casually insert their name into the first few sentences you speak, all the better.

The final part of the greeting is very subtle. It is not absolutely necessary, but it can work wonders on a subconscious level. After the introduction, lean in slightly in the direction of the person you are conversing with. This is body language that indicates your genuine interest in the person. Don't invade the person's personal space. The key to the lean is that if you are going to lean, you want it to be toward the person you are talking to. Leaning backward is the type of body language that suggests you are trying to exit the conversation as quickly as you can, which is the last thing that you want to project.

The handshake is an important piece of a first impression. As you've undoubtedly heard before, your handshake should be firm and respectful. No one likes a dead fish or bone crusher handshake. Eye contact is another essential part of the handshake. If you or someone you encounter prefers not to shake hands, try the "hands-free" handshake. This is a surprisingly effective alternative. Simply act as you normally would during a handshake but keep your hands at your side. Smile, make eye contact, introduce yourself, lean forward, and point your heart toward the person you are talking to. The same energy that you exude from a handshake can be put into a "hands-free" handshake.

Building Rapport

In any first conversation, the ultimate goal is to achieve rapport with someone. Rapport is the natural harmony that you feel with someone. You have a special rapport with your family members, friends, and work associates. You might find that you laugh at different things with different friends or speak in different cadences when around your mother compared to your boss. Rapport is a personal bond shared between people. Finding a rapport with someone is the first step of a fruitful relationship.

Contrary to popular belief, you can build a rapport with someone almost immediately. A great first impression will open the gates for a strong rapport to be formed. As a rapport builds, the person you're talking to will find themselves liking you and enjoying your company. It is natural for people to like other people that share their values, interests, and attitudes. When rapport is established, it is a natural connection that makes you feel in sync with the other person. Rapport also creates trust. When someone trusts you, they are much more likely to share things with you. Finding trust in someone will also cause your body to release the hormone oxytocin, also known as the love hormone.

Rapport starts with empathy. If you have the ability to put yourself in the shoes of the person you are talking to, you can accurately understand their emotions. It stands to reason that if you can understand someone's emotions, you can anticipate how your words or actions will make them feel. When you lead with empathy, a person's natural defensive state will drop. People are naturally skeptical of people they have never met. Showing empathy in any capacity will make the person you are talking with feel seen.

If empathy is the hero of rapport, then ego is the enemy. Always leave your ego at the door. When people carry too much ego, they tend to dominate conversations. This is not a good thing. Someone who dominates a conversation is most likely not listening to the person they are speaking to. A person with a big ego will continually turn the conversation back to themself. Most people do not like being talked over or listening to someone drone on about themselves. On the flip side of the coin, an insecure ego is just as harmful to rapport. Some people are so insecure that they can't handle a moment of silence. They will speak in scattered thoughts or voice every thought that comes into their head. This is another great way to blow your chances of building a solid rapport.

Perhaps you know someone that is a magician when it comes to building rapport with strangers. They can meet someone and within the first minute of conversation, they are talking like old friends. Like all masters of rapport, this person most likely has a useful attitude. A useful can-do attitude sounds like an old cliché, but it can be the difference-maker in building rapport. The next time you meet someone new, go into the conversation thinking about *what you want*, not *what you don't want*. Here's a great example: you are meeting someone who is about to interview you for a job that you really want. The attitude you should have is that of someone who knows what they want. You want the job. You want to build a rapport with the interviewer and impress them. You want to appear professional and knowledgeable. If you were to come into the interview with a useless attitude, this would be a disaster waiting to happen. I hope the interviewer doesn't hate me. I don't want to embarrass myself. I'm nervous and I don't want to be here. Your body language will naturally reflect the attitude that you are carrying. Don't let your attitude sabotage your chance at building rapport. (A useful attitude does not necessarily mean a positive attitude. See the Synchronization section below.)

A common mistake people make in first conversations is inserting information about themselves in unnatural points of the conversation. This all comes back to the concept of active listening, one of the cornerstones of reading people and building rapport. Let your ego dissolve. The conversation does not need to be about you. In fact, you should steer the topic of conversation toward the other person as much as possible. Why? You are trying to build rapport. You cannot develop rapport with someone you know nothing about. The best way to learn about someone is to get them to start talking about themselves.

If there is one thing you take away from this chapter, let it be this: *ask questions.* You can attempt to build rapport by making witty comments or cracking a joke, but this will see mixed results. Most people do not want to jump into joking mode with a complete stranger. A person might laugh, but they might not see an opening to join in a conversation. A question is a direct line of conversation. People have an innate desire to talk about something interesting and sound knowledgeable. Nothing is easier than talking about yourself. A question invites someone to start talking about themselves. They might even share something that can help you build a rapport. Need some ideas of what questions to ask? Here are five suggestions:

1. What's your name?
2. Where do you live?
3. Do you have a family?
4. What do you do for a living?
5. Do you have any hobbies?

These questions might seem awkward, but they are tried and true. They are quick and easy ways to get someone to reveal information about themselves. You might ask someone if they have a family, to which they reply they have five brothers and sisters. You come from a big family as well. Bingo. Now you have something in common and something to talk about. Look how easy that was to build up a little rapport right out of the gate.

These five questions are simple conversation starters, but you by no means need to stick to these questions. It all has to do with the context and the environment. Going up to a person at a crowded bar and asking where they live is not recommended. Truthfully, there is not a topic that is off the table when it comes to good questions. However, there are definitely good and bad questions. The difference between a good and bad question usually has to do with the way a question is phrased.

The best question you can ask someone is an open-ended question. The most common open-ended questions begin with the words *who, what, when, why, where,* and *how.* The idea of an open-ended question is that you are encouraging a person to reveal as much about themselves as possible. Closed-ended questions are a great way for a conversation to come to a screeching halt. Closed-ended questions will usually illicit a yes or no response. For example:

You: Do you come here often?
Stranger: No.

Swing and a miss. What question do you ask next? Tough to say. You're basically back to square one. You still don't know anything about the person you're talking to. When a conversation feels like an interview, you're in trouble. If you're constantly asking questions that illicit short responses, it will begin to seem like you're badgering a person. Try an open-ended question instead of a closed-ended one:

You: How often do you come here?
Stranger: It's my first time here. I'm from out of town.

Much better. You didn't give that person a chance to respond with yes or no. The amount of information they reveal about themselves will depend on their willingness to converse, but the open-ended question doesn't give them an easy out. Now that you know this person is from out of town, you have a piece of information that can be used to build rapport. Some logical next questions might be *Where are you from?* or *What brings you here?* At least now you have a clearer pathway for creating a conversation and building rapport.

You should also take care to avoid leading, assumptive, or compound questions. These types of questions are exactly as they sound. Any question that is built on an assumption could lead to a halt in conversation. People also have an innate ability to pick up on questions that are leading them to talk about something. Compound questions are multiple questions packed into one, which will almost always confuse a person. The purpose of asking questions is to invite the other person to talk about themselves and to find a natural course for the conversation.

Once you have found common ground with the person you are talking to, you are in a good position to build rapport. If you feel weird about asking questions and not saying anything about yourself, don't. People are more likely to ask questions as a form of reciprocation. When they realize that you have taken an interest in them and that they are talking about themselves a lot, they will want to reciprocate the interest and ask you questions. When you are asked questions, be open and honest about your interests and your life. Revealing information about yourself is just one more way for a connection to be built.

Tools that we have previously discussed such as active listening, empathy, and emotional intelligence are all huge aspects of effective conversation. Once you have found a way to incorporate all of these tools at once, you will be a master of building rapport.

Synchronization

People like people that act like themselves. This is an extremely important point to remember. You have a conversation with someone where you ask all the right questions and you both have tons in common. But why does it still feel like the other person is not falling into a good rapport with you? Was it something you said? It was much more likely something you did. While you can talk about a show you both love until the cows come home, if the body language between you and the person you are talking to is on two different wavelengths, you will very well fail to build that rapport.

Think about the child that mimics one of their parents. The young son who learns to love baseball at an early age because he sees how passionate his father is about the sport. The son might not be conscious of it, but he understands that a great way to earn his dad's attention is to act similarly to his father. His father most likely pushed baseball onto his son, and the son in turn understood that developing a love for baseball was a great way to earn his father's approval. Soon they're both yelling at the TV screen when their team makes a costly error. They might both throw their hands up in exasperation. The young boy is a miniature clone of his father.

This is a basic example of synchronization. Think about your friends. Perhaps you have a particular group of friends. Do you feel like you all have similarities, inside jokes, and unique ways of doing things? People like people like themselves. It is only natural for people that are close to each other to align their morals, beliefs, and actions with the groups they belong to.

People become excited when they spot commonalities in others. They buy things from salesmen that are like themselves. They hire people that are like themselves. They date people that are like themselves. People are more likely to take action when they see a piece of themselves within someone else. So how can you achieve synchronization with someone who you just met? How can you make yourself in sync with someone you know nothing about?

Attitude synchronization is a great first step. In the rapport section, we discussed bringing a useful attitude into a conversation. While more often than not this is an upbeat attitude, this is not always the case. Bringing a positive and upbeat attitude to a funeral could be a recipe for disaster. Your attitude would be completely out of sync with everyone you talk to. This does not mean that if you approach someone for the first time, you should guess their attitude and try to mimic it. Follow the guidelines for a great first impression that are outlined at the beginning of the chapter. You will be able to decipher a person's attitude the more you talk to them.

Mirroring is a cornerstone concept of synchronization. When two people have an excellent rapport, their body language will seem to be in perfect sync. The next time you are at a restaurant, see if you can spot a happy couple. They might lean in the same direction, cross their legs the same way, make the same hand gestures, and take sips from their drinks at the same time. This is unconscious mirroring. When two people share a bond, their body language seeks to become synchronized.

Intentionally mirroring someone's body language is a great way to develop synchronization. If you are trying it for the first time, take it slow, and don't force it. Maybe if a person you're speaking to shrugs their shoulders when they talk, you do the same. If a person puts their hands on their hips, put your hands on your hips. If you're thinking that this will be blatantly obvious to the person you are mirroring, you will be shocked at how wrong you are. The truth is that when most people are preoccupied with a conversation, they are not thinking about their body language. Body language is mostly read subconsciously, and mirroring is no exception. A person being mirrored isn't thinking *this person is a copycat*, but rather *there's something about this person.*

You can mirror someone by matching a head tilt, a gesture, posture, facial expressions, or breathing patterns. If someone sitting across from you is tapping their foot on the floor, match their rhythm with a toe tap. Just don't take it over the top and do it obviously. If someone mentions that they have a tooth ache and starts massaging their jaw, don't also start messaging your jaw. When someone calls attention to a piece of their body language, they are looking for you to weigh in on it, not to mimic it.

Verbal mirroring is another excellent tactic for creating synchronization. Matching someone's tone of voice is a great tactic to use. You should also attempt to match someone's volume and speed of talking. If someone is a quiet talker, don't use a booming voice while talking. People that talk quieter might be introverts. If you match their volume and tone, they will feel like they have made an immediate connection. You can also try using similar words as the person you are speaking with. If someone describes something as "cool," try using that word naturally in a sentence. Similar to body language, people will subconsciously notice and be attracted to people that speak like them. Just as friends might speak in the same slang or cadences, people are constantly on the lookout for people that are like them.

A quick disclaimer before we move on to the next chapter. You may feel like some of the tactics in this chapter seem manipulative or dishonest. That could not be further from the truth. Unless your goals are to make a connection with someone so you can take advantage of them, there is nothing wrong with using any of these tactics to have a terrific conversation. In fact, people will be happy you did. Everyone has a basic human need to connect with others. When someone makes a new connection and bonds with someone new, it is a great feeling.

If you use open-ended questions or mirroring during your next first encounter, don't feel like you're cheating. If you make a true connection with someone, you would likely have made the connection anyway had you had more time. But with most encounters, you don't have much time to make an impression.

The Art of Speed-Reading People

We've now reached the exciting part. In this chapter, you will bring together the skills that have been highlighted earlier, and you will learn how to use these skills to speed-read people. What exactly does it mean to speed-read people? Speed-reading is the art of identifying a person's personality type simply by observing them.

The benefits of identifying a person's personality are endless. Speed-reading can help you become a better manager, salesperson, spouse, parent, or general communicator. When you know a person's personality type you can communicate with them in their preferred method of communication. You can present ideas in a way that they are sure to be receptive to. You can spot their natural strengths and weaknesses. Speed-reading is a skill reserved for a top-tier communicator.

Recall from Chapter 3 that there are four personality spectrums and eight personality traits. A person can be introverted (I) or extroverted (E), a sensor (S) or an intuitive (N), a thinker (T) or a feeler (F), and a judger (J) or a perceiver (P). Depending on where a person falls on these four spectrums will determine their personality type. There are also four temperament types, which are equally useful to identify. People of similar temperaments tend to communicate in the same way. The four temperaments are traditionalists (sensing judgers), experiencers (sensing perceivers), conceptualizers (intuitive thinkers), and idealists (intuitive feelers). Revisit

Chapter 3 if you need a refresher on the personality spectrums or temperaments.

The purpose of this chapter is not to give you a superhuman ability to spot personality types. There will be times when a person's exact personality type will not be clear to you. If you can identify two of the four personality traits in someone, you are already much better equipped to communicate with them effectively. The trick is to start with what you are certain about. If you are certain a person is extroverted but unsure whether they are a sensor or an intuitive, then start with their extrovert trait and work from there. Be sure not to rush to judgment. Take your time and be willing to take in new information about a person at all times. You might find something out about a person that modifies your preexisting diagnosis. It is also important that you familiarize yourself with your own biases. Your personality type may leave you predisposed to certain biases.

Before we begin to break down the characteristics of each personality type, let's try an example exercise. Read the following scenario carefully. Use context clues and details about Mrs. Stevenson to help you determine her personality type.

Mrs. Stevenson is the 55-year-old teacher of your son's sixth-grade class. You are currently walking into a parent-teacher conference with Mrs. Stevenson. You are walking into the conference with a bone to pick: Mrs. Stevenson recently gave your son a C- on a paper that he worked all week on. When you get into Mrs. Stevenson's office you notice that her desk is neat and tidy, with very little clutter. She has your son's file of schoolwork placed front and center on her desk.

She also has two pictures of her own children on her desk, along with a homemade mug from one of her students that reads "Best Teacher Ever." Mrs. Stevenson is dressed professionally, with lovely hair and modest jewelry. Mrs. Stevenson greets you with a smile and apologizes that the conference before yours went late. When Mrs. Stevenson talks about your son, she speaks respectfully and kindly. Although your son is known for being a troublemaker, Mrs. Stevenson chooses to pick out the areas in which he has improved this year, choosing to focus on strengths over weaknesses. When she does mention things that your son can improve on, she is very specific, and sites thorough examples of why your son has misbehaved or struggled. She speaks energetically and makes animated hand gestures to make her points. She occasionally looks over to the door when someone passes by, but she keeps the majority of her attention on you. When you bring up the frustration you have about the C- grade your son received, Mrs. Stevenson nods and listens attentively. When you are finished, Mrs. Stevenson says that she understands why you would be upset by the grade. Mrs. Stevenson then walks you through her rigorous grading rubric and how she arrived at that grade for your son's paper. You get the impression that Mrs. Stevenson is very serious about her role as a teacher, but she is genuinely concerned about her students and empathizes with your frustration.

Question 1: Does Mrs. Stevenson seem like an introvert or extrovert?

Clues: Mrs. Stevenson is energetic and personable. She seems very comfortable dealing with people. She is also an animated talker who uses hand gestures. While she is attentively talking to you, she also notices the people walking by her door, which indicates she is aware of the activity going on around her.

Answer: Mrs. Stevenson is most likely an extrovert.

You now can eliminate eight of the sixteen personality types for Mrs. Stevenson. Let's continue to build off that.

Question 2: Does Mrs. Stevenson seem like a sensor or an intuitive?

Clues: Mrs. Stevenson is very specific and precise. When she talks about your son's weaknesses as a student, she does not use generalities, but rather specific examples. She also gives you a detailed breakdown of her grading rubric. Her attitude indicated she is living very much in the moment.

Answer: Mrs. Stevenson is likely a sensor.

You now know that Mrs. Stevenson is one of four personalities: ESTJ, ESTP, ESFJ, or ESFP.

Question 3: Does Mrs. Stevenson seem like a feeler or a thinker?

Clues: Mrs. Stevenson is friendly and personable. She also showcases her extreme empathy multiple times throughout the conversation. She takes great care to focus on the positives about your son, rather than hammer home the misbehavior and bad grades. When you express frustration over the C-, Mrs. Stevenson expresses that she understands why you would be frustrated. She also openly displays pictures of her own children on her desk.

Answer: Mrs. Stevenson is likely a feeler.

This leaves ESFJ and ESFP.

Question 4: Does Mrs. Stevenson seem like a judger or a perceiver?

Clues: Mrs. Stevenson's desk is neat and orderly. Everything she says within the conference is decisive and purposeful. When you mention the C-, although Mrs. Stevenson expresses empathy, she is also quick to walk you step-by-step through her grading rubric. It would seem that she has a by-the-book attitude. She also apologized for the conference before yours running late, which suggests she is conscious of her schedule.

Answer: Mrs. Stevenson is most likely a Judger.

This would make Mrs. Stevenson an ESFJ. This personality type is sometimes referred to as the Consul. Consuls are attentive, people-focused, and live by strict values.

Let's try one more method of determining Mrs. Stevenson's personality type. Let's start over and try using the temperaments as a method of speed-reading Mrs. Stevenson.

Question 5: What temperament best fits Mrs. Stevenson?

Clues: Mrs. Stevenson is very well organized and presents herself very carefully. The conference appears to be well planned out, and she is decisive about her teaching strategies. This would eliminate an experiencer temperament.

Mrs. Stevenson does not think about your son as if he was another name on her grade sheet. She is attuned to his idiosyncrasies. She does not look at teaching from an analytical or theoretical point of view, but rather seems to personally invest in her students. This would eliminate the conceptual temperament.

She also appears to be very much present in the moment. Your son is the focus of the conversation, and she does not break off into tangents or lose interest. She is very specific with details about your son and does not put your son into the context of a bigger picture. This would eliminate the idealist temperament.

Answer: Mrs. Stevenson is most likely a traditionalist.

This means her personality type is either ESTJ, ESFJ, ISTJ, or ISFJ. The same information that we used to determine that Mrs. Stevenson is a traditionalist will help us determine her personality type. Simply put, Mrs. Stevenson appears to extrovert her feelings. This would leave ESFJ as the only logical option.

Do you think you have the hang of it? If not, that's okay. The more you practice with people, the more your skills will develop. People are complex, and it is very common for some people to appear as if they could fall on either side of a spectrum. The more information you compile, the better formed your decision will be. We will now take a deeper dive into the four temperaments and the sixteen personality types. Each personality type has its quirks and patterns. If you're perceptive enough, you might be able to spot a personality type with just one look.

Traditionalists

Traditionalists are also known as the sensing judgers. This is a useful moniker to remember traditionalists because all traditionalists have the sensing and judging traits. This means that a traditionalist could be extroverted or introverted. They might also be a thinker or a feeler. This means that while traditionalists share a lot of commonalities, there can also be wide differences. As sensing judgers, traditionalists like to live in the here and now. They are very attuned to themselves and those around them. They are decisive and detail oriented. They appreciate order and structure in their lives. They carry themselves with dignity and show respect for others.

There are some general communication strategies that tend to work on all traditionalist types. Traditionalists appreciate people that are direct and straightforward in the way they communicate. During a serious conversation with a traditionalist, don't use a joke to lighten the mood. A traditionalist might take this as a sign that you are not taking the conversation as seriously as they are. Being well-structured, traditionalists appreciate when you are well prepared and organized. Showing up late and unprepared to a meeting with a traditionalist could have a disastrous effect on further communication efforts. Present information to a traditionalist in sequential order. Traditionalists prefer specific, direct, and well-structured information. Avoid talking in long, roundabout ways with a traditionalist. This would likely lead a traditionalist to feel like you are wasting their time. If you know the traditionalist you are talking to, it might be beneficial to mention their values. Traditionalists typically live by stern values, and they look for those same values in others.

ESTJs

The ESTJ personality type is also often referred to as the Executive. They are natural-born leaders who can offer a calming force among their peers or subordinates. They think logically and analytically and thrive when they have to make decisions. ESTJs are highly ethical people who seldom play favorites. Highly competitive, controlling, and strong-willed, the Executive can sometimes come off as callous. This is because feeling is their *least function*, meaning it is the personality trait that they are least attuned with. ESTJs are also extremely focused on the present, which may cause them to have a blind spot in areas of the future.

If you were trying to spot an ESTJ in a crowd, you would look for someone who is dressed neat and conservative. An ESTJ's appearance and actions are always appropriate for any occasion. They might be friendly and physically animated, but they rarely converse on an emotional level. ESTJ's also have a high energy level. Because they love taking leadership roles, they are the first to volunteer to lead new projects. It is not unusual for an ESTJ to appear bossy or controlling.

The best strategy for communicating with an ESTJ is to be assertive. ESTJs make decisions quickly, logically, and without emotion. An ESTJ will respect people that exhibit a strong will and forceful opinion (as long as it is backed by strong logic). Don't worry about offending an ESTJ. ESTJs don't take things personally, and you shouldn't take criticism or a blunt comment from an ESTJ personally either. Trying to appeal to an ESTJ with an emotional plea will be a lost cause. The more logical, data-driven, and realistic an argument, the more likely an ESTJ will side with you. As with all traditionalists, it is best to speak to them directly. Never beat around the bush with an Executive.

Introverts might struggle to comprehend the confidence and quick decisions an ESTJ makes. Intuitives might struggle to get ESTJs to look toward the future. When intuitives make plans for the future that are detailed and organized, they are much more likely to get the attention of an ESTJ. Perceivers won't be able to relate to the decisiveness of the ESTJ because they like to leave their options open. When perceivers can explain the logical benefits of multiple options and backup plans, ESTJs will listen. Feelers will have the most trouble communicating with ESTJs. Feelers need to take a step back and think as objectively as possible when communicating with an Executive.

ISTJs

ISTJs are also known as Logisticians. ISTJs are responsible, hardworking, no-nonsense people. Their strongest function is sensing, which gives them a unique ability to observe the specific details of day-to-day life. They are also gifted with impressive memories, often able to recall minute details about events from years ago. Logisticians are extremely conscientious and respectful. ISTJs get their work completely done before they even think about taking time to relax. Quiet and serious, Logisticians spend their downtime working on projects with their hands or enjoying nature. An ISTJ's least function is intuition, which often makes them conservative and distrusting of new ways of doing things. They are logical decision-makers that are always decisive and sometimes stubborn. Logisticians are eminently fair.

A Logistician's appearance and mannerisms will be dominated by their strait-laced nature. ISTJs dress conservatively and will most likely avoid loud colors. They will speak slowly and deliberately and will speak in precise details. ISTJs value their privacy, so they will rarely be caught talking about their personal life or emotions. Deliberate and methodical, the expression "slow and steady wins the race" is a perfect metaphor for the work style of the ISTJ. Their ultra-responsible lifestyle also makes them extremely disinclined to be caught in risky situations of any kind.

When communicating with an ISTJ, make sure to supply them with as many facts and details as possible. Express ideas in practical manners and when possible, mention past implementations of projects that ISTJs can reference. ISTJs will appreciate sequential plans with realistic schedules. Logisticians hate being rushed, so it is important to allow them adequate time to thoughtfully consider ways in which they can get a job done. Simplify the information that you relay to an ISTJ and they will thank you for it. When arguing with an ISTJ, stick to facts and logic. Emotional pleas will fall on deaf ears to a Logistician.

The thought-out and methodical approach that Logisticians use might not make sense to an extrovert. Extroverts should avoid putting pressure on Logisticians to make quick decisions. Feelers can speak ISTJ if they use logic and reason as opposed to emotion. Perceivers will likely respect the deliberate nature in which ISTJs weigh options and chart the best course, but they will also need to understand that once an ISTJ reaches a decision, it will be extremely difficult to change their mind. Perceivers that can speak cool and logically might be able to sway ISTJs. Intuitives will struggle the most with ISTJs. While intuitives like to make grand plans, think about the big picture, and try new methods of doing things, this is not at all how ISTJs think. When communicating with Logisticians, intuitives should keep their ideas as realistic as possible and be prepared for critiques of any real concerns that a Logistician will spot.

ESFJs

Often referred to as Consuls, ESFJs might be the friendliest and most outgoing of all the personality types. Extroverted feelers, the Consul values their family and friends above all else. Known for their generosity and loyalty, ESFJs will often give freely of themselves for those closest to them, and their community at large. ESFJs are sensitive people that have an innate need to be liked and appreciated by those around them. They have a strict sense of their personal values and code of behavior, and while they will likely follow this code closely, they might also try and instill these values in others. Consuls' least function is thinking, which will often hinder them from looking at a situation objectively and can lead to them getting their feelings hurt often. ESFJs are often down-to-earth and realistic, who treat life as serious business. Organized and productive workers, ESFJs value routine and are often averse to change.

ESFJs are often extremely polite and proper. They give themselves away by their affection. They will often physically demonstrate their friendliness with a pumping handshake, touching arms or shoulders, or giving warm hugs. They rarely try to hide their emotions, and their faces are often accurate reflections of their feelings. They are also often vocal about their values and might make suggestive comments about what they think someone else "should" do. ESFJs are quick to volunteer for projects and might act controlling of the details to achieve what they believe will be the "best" outcome.

When communicating with an ESFJ, you should always try to respect their feelings. Telling them that they are acting irrationally will only succeed in hurting them further. You should always attempt to find common ground with an ESFJ before you criticize them. If you are not careful in the way you criticize them, they might get offended. Consuls are run by their values, so it is important not to suggest a course of action that would directly go against those values. Be explicit and genuine by letting ESFJs know when you appreciate something they have done.

Introverts may struggle to keep up with the quick and long-talking ESFJs. As long as introverts are comfortable flexing their listening skills, ESFJs are finely attuned to others' emotions and won't overburden an introvert. Intuitives may have a hard time accepting a Consul's tendency to stick with old habits and beliefs rather than trying new things. Intuitives will need to show ESFJs that the effort it will take to try something new will be worth it. Similarly, perceivers may find ESFJs stubbornness stifling, and they should try their hardest to meet the expectations that are clearly set by ESFJs. Thinkers will need to be the most cautious when talking with ESFJs. They will find it hard to understand Consuls' habits of taking things personally and getting easily offended. Once an ESFJ's feelings are hurt or they believe someone has crossed a line, they may write someone off completely.

ISFJs

ISFJs are sometimes called Defenders. ISFJs are hardworking, thoughtful, and devoted. Defenders are motivated most by their need to belong, and they are valued members of any club or group they join. ISFJs' lead function is sensing, and thus they devote all their energy and attention to the problem in front of them. They are incredibly accurate with facts, have a knack for details, and often have steel-trap memories. While they are often reserved people, they are fiercely loyal family members and friends. ISFJs hate confrontation and will accommodate people that are upset. They will almost always avoid an argument. Their least function is intuition, so naturally, ISFJs struggle imagining scenarios that do not exist or working on a task without prior knowledge. Their kind and generous nature will often lead them into trouble, as people might try and take advantage of them.

ISFJs are modest and polite people that will not often call attention to themselves. You might find them working behind the scenes and giving their all to a volunteer organization. You might be able to spot an ISFJ if they exhibit any of their impressive recall. They are often quiet people, and their body language is reserved. ISFJs will faithfully follow the rules, work hard, and fly under the radar. They are also intensely private people who do not enjoy sharing details about their private life.

When talking with an ISFJ, make sure to be specific with what you want. An ISFJ's ability to catch every detail will make them appreciate conversation that is explicit and doesn't beat around the bush. It is also important to respect their privacy. Do not share information about an ISFJ with other people without their permission. If they reveal a piece of personal information to you, it is because they trust you, and that information was meant for you and you alone. Defenders appreciate people that speak with the same energy as their own: polite, nice, low volume, and respectful. Don't interrupt a Defender when they are talking. Give them ample time to respond to questions and think over their words.

Extroverts might be impatient by the slow and reserved manner in which ISFJs speak. By being patient, they can find ISFJs very easy to communicate with. Thinkers might judge ISFJs as not tough enough, mistaking the sensitivity of the Defender as weakness. Perceivers might also struggle with getting ISFJs to act spontaneously. By giving an ISFJ more information ahead of time, they can plan accordingly and live more spontaneously. Intuitives might find it the most frustrating to communicate with Defenders because of the ISFJ's inability to see the bigger picture. When intuitives slow down and listen carefully to ISFJs, they will find a charming and thoughtful soul.

Experiencers

The four experiencer personalities are all sensing perceivers. Like traditionalists, their sensing function allows them to always live in the present and be hyperaware of their surroundings. Where experiencers differ from traditionalists is that they are perceivers instead of judgers. This makes experiencers much more open to new ideas, activities, and occupations. Experiencers are often referred to as "free spirits." They value their freedom more than anything. They rarely worry about the future, instead choosing to put all their energy into the here and now.

Some general tips should be followed when you communicate with one of the experiencers. Be friendly and open with experiencers, as this is how they tend to communicate. Experiencers are very much attuned to reality, so focusing conversation on the immediate moment is always preferred. Experiencers also appreciate people that can be casual and not take themselves too seriously. They enjoy mixing business with pleasure. Avoid lecturing experiencers, and instead, try to entertain them as much as possible. They will be captivated if you can offer variety, thrills, or lively conversation.

ESTPs

ESTPs are often referred to as Entrepreneurs. The ESTP treats life like one great adventure. They are incredibly attuned to their surroundings and are constantly active and curious. They are adaptable and will often go with the flow, oftentimes not considering the consequences of their decisions. They pair their seize-the-day energy with realistic expectations and impulsivity. They are full of energy, love surprises, and are willing to participate in most activities as long as they don't get too intense. The Entrepreneur's least function is intuition, so when conversations get too theoretical or serious, they tend to tune out or try to turn the conversation to humor. Their restless nature makes ESTPs great athletes. Their easygoing and casual nature often leads them to be popular or flirtatious, otherwise known as "the life of the party." Because they are thinkers and not feelers, they might give the false impression that they care more about someone than they actually do.

To adequately speed-read an ESTP, it is always preferable to observe the person in more than one environment. ESTPs are sometimes referred to as "chameleons" because they can adapt so easily to any environment. Look for signs of outgoingness, energetic attitudes, and a gregarious nature if you suspect someone of being an ESTP. Although they prefer casual clothing that can work well in any situation, their keen awareness of how other people perceive them makes them quite stylish. ESTPs know how to work a room and may be friends with everyone at the party.

When communicating with an ESTP, don't be afraid to engage with them and participate in a good-natured exchange of ideas. Don't take yourself too seriously when conversing with an entrepreneur. A good-natured ribbing from an ESTP should be taken only as a joke, and they love when you engage in light jokes and chop-busting. Like all thinkers, they will respond more strongly to ideas based in pragmatism rather than emotion. Present your ideas to an ESTP simply and in a straightforward manner. They are also prone to modify plans and take risks if they see the move as logical, so don't be afraid to play into their sense of adventure.

Introverts might become frustrated by the ESTP's lack of interest in extensive exploration into a topic. Introverts' best method for communication with an ESTP might be a written condensed summary, especially in the workplace. Feelers will have trouble understanding the ESTP's habit of not taking serious matters to heart the way feelers do. They may also mistake the extroverted behavior of the Entrepreneur as an emotional connection that isn't there. Judgers will not be able to relate to the spontaneity of the ESTP. Appealing to the thinker function of the Entrepreneur is the best bet for judgers. Intuitives will face the biggest hurdle in communication with the Entrepreneur because of how hard it is to make ESTPs see the bigger picture. Using comparisons to past successful ventures will help ESTPs see the logical side of long-term plans.

ISTPs

ISTPs are also known as Virtuosos. The Virtuoso is known for their extreme independence and vision. ISTPs are unwavering in times of extreme pressure and seem to always be calm and collected. They are extremely resourceful and preceptive people that often have a knack for mechanics. Being introverted thinkers, they rarely have time for people that they deem irrational or overly emotional. Virtuosos value privacy over anything else. Practical, realistic, and adaptable, virtuosos love tackling any problem that comes their way, but they'd prefer to go it alone. ISTPs are also known to be risk-takers and adrenaline junkies. They prefer people that are direct and honest and have no patience for people with hidden agendas. Similar to Entrepreneurs, the Virtuoso's least function is feeling. Because they thrive in privacy, they can often appear closed off and emotionally inaccessible to others.

ISTPs are reserved by nature, which makes them difficult to speed-read. While an ISTP might not willingly reveal much of themselves to others, their interests and hobbies are a great tip-off. ISTPs love spending time with machines or engaging in physical activities and would much rather do either of these things than engage with people. ISTPs are not particularly concerned about what other people think about them, and their clothing choices reflect this. ISTPs will choose clothing that is comfortable and functional. An ISTP's risk-taking nature will also reveal itself in their jobs and hobbies. Typical jobs of ISTPs include police officers, firefighters, construction, or emergency medical professions. Hobbies often include physical challenges or extreme sports.

When communicating with an ISTP, it is best not to be pushy. If an ISTP feels their space is being violated, they will not appreciate it. It is best to be pragmatic when talking with an ISTP. If you can make suggestions or requests that are well thought out and logical, ISTPs will respond well. Free time and spontaneity are highly valued by ISTPs, so it is best to be explicit about what you want from them and try not to overschedule their time. Don't use emotion to appeal to an ISTP. They will feel like they are being guilted into something. There is no need to heap excessive praise on an ISTP because it means next to nothing to them. You should also listen carefully when conversing with a Virtuoso. They are not likely to repeat themselves.

Extraverts often become frustrated by the intense privacy of an ISTP. ISTPs are motivated by action. Extraverts should appeal to this love of action to get ISTPs on board with a mission. Intuitives might be baffled by Virtuosos thrill-seeking moment-to-moment lifestyle. Speaking logically to Virtuosos will help them to see the importance of unforeseen factors that might arise from their actions. Judgers will also struggle with ISTPs' unwillingness to work within narrowly set boundaries. Judgers will have to understand the ISTP's need for independence in order to best understand them. ISTPs are most productive when they feel a sense of ownership over a project. Feelers may also be off put by the shortness of Virtuosos. It takes a long time to forge a connection with an ISTP. Feelers should not take offense at an ISTP's disinterest in an emotional relationship.

ESFPs

ESFPs are also called the Entertainers. They enjoy being the center of attention and delighting everyone they are with. They are warm, outgoing, and vivacious people by nature. They are social creatures that enjoy making connections with other social people. Entertainers are usually animated and fun-loving, and like all experiencers, they very much live in the moment. Their least function is intuition, which means they are not very skilled at predicting future events. They live busy social lives and will often overextend themselves because of their many friends and their preference for living in the present moment. Entertainers are generous and curious; they rarely enter a situation with a preconceived notion. Their feeler function separates them from ESTPs because they are much more likely to get their feelings hurt.

ESFPs are open and friendly people. They exude an approachable nature that makes people attracted to them. They thrive when they are the center of attention, which means they might be the person at the party who starts playing an instrument or telling a story. ESFPs live in the moment and are not particularly complicated people. They will speak in a straightforward matter with clear and concise language. They will ask questions of other people and express genuine interest in most people they interact with. You will not find an ESFP sitting around having a serious conversation. They prefer action or busy social events.

When talking with an ESFP, do not speak in hypotheticals. They prefer conversations grounded in reality and the present. ESFPs tend to speak in a casual easygoing manner. If possible, do not become overly serious with an ESFP. When presenting ideas to ESFPs, speak about the practical way in which it will help others. It is also important to respect an ESFP's privacy. Just because they are extremely friendly and gregarious does not mean they want to divulge personal details about their life. If you need to criticize an ESFP, make sure to include a compliment with a criticism. ESFPs respond great to surprises, and they enjoy making games and adventures out of everyday activities.

Introverts might find ESFPs too talkative for their own personal style. They may need to be prepared to speak immediately about their thoughts or opinions on a matter. Introverts will benefit from keeping their thoughts brief and to the point when talking to an ESFP. Thinkers might consider ESFPs too sensitive. Thinkers need to understand the emotional function of the ESFP that drives them to help others. Judgers may become frustrated by the Entertainer's inability to make a decision and stick to it. Judgers should emphasize that the quicker a decision is made, the more convenient it will be for everyone involved. Intuitives will find the realistic aspects of the ESFP to be hindering to their ideas. If intuitives want ESFPs to accept their new or innovative ideas, they should stress the altruism of their ideas.

ISFPs

ISFPs can be referred to as Adventurers. They are gentle and sensitive souls that care deeply for others. Adventurers are as unassuming and down-to-earth as it gets. They are often quiet people who communicate with very few words. They are deeply loyal to their family and friends and would prefer to demonstrate their loyalty through actions rather than words. ISFPs are lead feelers, which means they tend to take most things personally. They can often appear cool and detached to others, but make no mistake, they feel everything that others experience. They are deeply selective about who they take into their confidence. Being sensors, they are highly observant of their surroundings and may overextend themselves in their need to help others that they perceive to be hurting. Unassertive and docile, they look to maintain harmony and avoid conflict. Adventurers assume the best in people. Adventurers enjoy the simple things in life, prioritizing family and friends over work.

To spot an ISFP, you should look for a quiet and modest person. They are affectionate with the people they know; however, they might appear cool to those they don't. They are typically very relaxed people and have no problem going with the flow. You will not catch an ISFP in an argument trying to persuade someone of something. ISFPs do not particularly care what other people do with their lives, and they see no point in trying to control them. On the flip side of this coin, ISFPs will go to any lengths necessary to please the people that are important to them. They will likely wear clothes that are casual and comfortable. They might use a hand gesture or facial expression to communicate as opposed to their words.

When communicating with an ISFP, it is important to respect their privacy and avoid being pushy. ISFPs tend to be turned off by people that are loud, boisterous, or argumentative. It is important to be specific and not beat around the bush with an Adventurer. You can also appeal to their innate desire to help others, which will surely be great motivation for them. Because they do not like to be pushed, you should give ISFPs ample time to react to new information or proposals. Being sensors, they appreciate ideas that are built in practicality rather than imagination. They are also happy to give their opinion, and while they may politely acknowledge yours, don't make the mistake of thinking that they agree with you because they do not argue against your point.

Extroverts will often find it difficult to get ISFPs moving on a project. Extroverts should understand that ISFPs need adequate time to think things over and being rushed won't help. Intuitives might struggle with getting ISFPs to see the long-term consequences of their decisions or attempting to get ISFPs to see the bigger picture. Intuitives should demonstrate how their plans will help people in the present as well as in the future. Judgers might become inconvenienced by ISFPs who do not feel compelled to stick to any given plan. Judgers should avoid labeling ISFPs as indecisive, and instead try to gently persuade ISFPs with small and easy steps. Thinkers will likely clash with Adventurers the most because they will not understand the sensitivity of Adventurers. They should remember when they speak to ISFPs that they are talking to someone that values people's feelings over everything else.

Conceptualizers

The intuitive thinkers, conceptualizers are very different from both traditionalists and experiencers. These logical people like to look at things from the big picture. They are often looking toward the future, and love developing big and innovative plans. Because they prefer logic over emotion, these thinkers are known to be objective decision-makers. They value competence in people. They set big goals for themselves and try to excel at everything. They are creative people with a love for problem-solving.

If you suspect someone of being a conceptualizer, there are some general tips for communication that can be of great help. Conceptualizers love to be intellectually stimulated. Their curious nature makes them always game for a theoretical discussion. Conceptualizers aren't too worried about specifics; talk to them in terms of the larger implications of things. Conceptualizers like to have their imagination piqued, so talking about ideas of concepts that are out of the norm will excite conceptualizers. Conceptualizers respond well to confidence, so try and present your ideas with gusto and enthusiasm. Don't bore them with details; for conceptualizers, details can always be ironed out later. Appeal to their logic and sense of fairness. Also, it is important that you are not afraid to show a conceptualizer your competence. They will respect you greatly when you show them that you are knowledgeable on a given topic.

ENTJs

ENTJs are also known as Commanders. They have a natural ability to lead, and they inspire others to follow. Like all conceptualizers, they have a unique ability to think analytically and critically about big decisions. Commanders value honesty, and they will often speak bluntly and get right to the point. The least function of the ENTJ is feeling, which makes them frequently oblivious to the emotions of others. They can also come off as arrogant and bossy because they have little patience for people that struggle to comprehend things as quickly as they do. ENTJs have a knack for strategic planning and innovative thinking. Their ability to think quickly, exude natural energy, and attain vast knowledge often makes them gifted public speakers. Often career driven, ENTJs keep things organized and are always productive. They might also be negligent to the direct consequences of their actions, as their minds are always thinking toward the future.

Commanders can often be spotted quickly because they have no problem making themselves known and seen. They will appear friendly and outgoing, and they talk fast because they think fast. Their movements and body language will appear brisk and purposeful. They are very quick learners and have no problem comprehending complex concepts that you might hurl at them. Their confidence in themselves will strike many as arrogance. They might also inadvertently talk down to people who they perceive as not on their intellectual level, so their words can often seem condescending. They will speak with a dense vocabulary.

When speaking to an ENTJ, be direct and purposeful. It is also important that you follow through on any promises that you make to an ENTJ. ENTJs have a grand and specific vision, and they rely on others to make it happen. You should do your homework before talking to an ENTJ. They have no problem picking arguments and challenging your knowledge. While they may be intimidating, you should always stand your ground and be decisive when talking to an ENTJ. Don't worry about hurting their feelings. If you have a well-thought-out plan that is innovative and creative, this can be music to an ENTJ's ears. If an ENTJ hurts your feelings, it was likely inadvertently. The best thing you can do is address what the ENTJ did immediately and let them know what exactly it was that hurt you.

Introverts will likely be challenged by the ENTJ's quick-moving and bold actions. ENTJs value knowledge and expertise, so if they view an introvert as being adequately knowledgeable, they will often consult them in their ventures. Sensors will likely see the big ideas of an ENTJ as impractical and unrealistic. They can convince ENTJs about the importance of the details if they stress that it will benefit the larger idea. Perceivers will likewise be turned off by the decisive nature of the Commander which may come across as stubbornness. The more they use logic, the more likely they are to get the ENTJ to see their point of view. Feelers will find it hardest to communicate with ENTJs. The ENTJ will often say and act in ways that seem to be deliberately hurtful to feelers. Feelers need to understand that rude comments from an ENTJ are intended as helpful and constructive criticism, and there was no malice behind the ENTJ's words.

INTJs

INTJs are often referred to as Architects. Much like ENTJs, INTJs are known for their original minds that have the ability to think on a global scale. Their lead intuition function allows them to see connections, hidden implications, and innovative methods that are invisible to everyone else. INTJs are always on a quest for improvement. They place a high priority on their intelligence and competence. They are flowing with creativity and imagination. Their ability to problem-solve and think critically is second to none. The Architect's least function is sensing, which often means that they struggle to participate in the real world. INTJs are most interested in what is going on in their heads, and thus they are often aloof to their physical surroundings. They are often thinking in intellectual or technical terms and thus will fail to be attuned to other people's emotions. Like Commanders, Architects can come off as condescending to people due to their vast array of knowledge and inattention to emotions. Due to their introverted nature, INTJs prefer to work alone on their own projects.

When speed-reading an INTJ, you will likely observe someone who is cool and reserved when around others. INTJs might give themselves away when asked about their personal projects or ventures. They will likely talk very excitedly about their projects or areas where they have a large amount of knowledge. INTJs also often talk in long complicated sentences that can confuse listeners. The Architect's mind is constantly churning out new ideas, concepts, and connections, and when they speak, they might not realize that they are leaving others behind. They often dress conservatively but can also have a unique look. This is because they are unconcerned with how others perceive them. The high standards they set for themselves are often placed on others, making them demanding bosses or parents.

In order to strike up effective communication with an INTJ, you should submit new ideas to them in writing. Give them time to conceptualize the ideas that you propose. INTJs like to hear the strategy that they can use to implement an idea, so when possible, talk in these terms. There is no need to heap praise on an Architect. They find cheerleading unnecessary and might even find it insulting if you overdo it. Do not attempt to finish an INTJ's sentences; instead let them complete their thoughts, no matter how rambling they may be. You should present arguments logically as opposed to emotionally. Talk to an INTJ in terms of the big picture and they are likely to respond positively.

Extroverts will be challenged by the INTJ's desire to delve deep into issues for long periods of time. They should realize that the more patient they are with the INTJ, the better the final product of their work. Feelers might find INTJs to be cold in the way they are oblivious of other people. They should not take comments or criticism from an INTJ literally. They should also not expect verbal approval from an INTJ. Silence indicates consent for an INTJ. Perceivers will also find INTJs tough and stubborn people to convince. They should speak logically to an INTJ and always meet a deadline set by an INTJ. There is no point in trying to get an INTJ to be more accommodating to you, so it is best to give them the space they desire. Sensors will find it hardest to speak with INTJs because of the INTJs endless creativity. Sensors should avoid discounting INTJs' radical ideas.

ENTPs

ENTPs are known as Debaters. Their extroversion helps them to be extremely sociable and charming people. ENTPs are incredibly skillful at the art of communication and make great impressions on people. They are lead intuitives, making them highly creative, with a knack for seeing the big picture. They love anticipating trends, taking risks, and getting others to join in on their venture. They are excellent persuaders, negotiators, and confidence boosters. Their least function is sensing, which means they are often blind to the practicality of an idea. This also leads to many ideas that never come to fruition because of a lack of attention to the details. ENTPs love the thrill of chasing after a goal, while the actual accomplishment of the goal itself is less exciting. Curious, open-minded, and highly flexible, ENTPs like to keep their options open. ENTPs can run the risk of becoming chronic procrastinators. They must rely on their keen intellect to recognize their destructive tendencies.

When looking for an ENTP, take notice of people that you find charming, sociable, and even flirtatious. They thoroughly enjoy being around people and have no problem stepping into the spotlight. You will likely find an ENTP to be a master communicator; great at telling stories and jokes. They always have a new scheme or plan that they are eager to hatch. In conversations with an ENTP, notice their confident and friendly body language. They will have no problem initiating physical contact with a shoulder touch, and they will often talk closely with people. Because ENTPs are highly aware of how other people perceive them, they will often be dressed in stylish or expensive clothes. Their impulsivity means that they are always game for a spontaneous adventure, even if it means neglecting other duties.

ENTPs are always enthusiastic about new ideas, so when you talk with them, be prepared to take any new ideas and explore them in-depth. A Debater is also likely to ask you a lot of questions, so be ready to answer them. If you are trying to persuade an ENTP, be sure to emphasize how your plan or logic is unique. Like most intuitives, ENTPs do not want to hear about the details, they want to hear about the big picture. Be flexible and open to suggestions when working with an ENTP. They might want to put their personal touch on a project. ENTPs enjoy having many different options as opposed to just one. ENTPs will respond well to you if you give them time to think about their various ventures, and also are open-minded enough to discuss their ideas with them.

Challenges may arise in communication between introverts and ENTPs. Debaters move quickly and like to talk a lot, so introverts should anticipate many questions and back-and-forth before entering a conversation with an ENTP. Feelers may feel a strong connection with an ENTP, only to get hurt emotionally when they discover that the emotional connection, they feel is one-sided. Feelers should realize that ENTPs are people pleasers, and they often overextend themselves with the things they say to people. Judgers will likely become annoyed at the ENTP's inability to make a decision and stick with it. Their best strategy would be to gently nudge ENTPs toward making a decision. Sensors will likely have trouble relating to the creative imagination or the

Debater, potentially seeing them as unrealistic. They should learn to appreciate the gifts of the ENTP, while also nurturing them toward a decision.

INTPs

INTPs are sometimes called the Logicians. These lead thinkers govern their lives by logic and analysis. Their introverted function makes them lovers of alone time where they can brainstorm, solve problems, and mull over new ideas. INTPs are often perfectionists in pursuit of the perfect way to accomplish a task. INTPs search out creative challenges. People may perceive them as complex or detached. INTPs have a unique ability to act calmly under any sort of pressure. They are also rarely intimidated. Logicians are intrigued by power and are always thinking on global scales, while typically ignoring details they find mundane. Feeling is their least function, so they will often come off to others as arrogant in the way that they prioritize ideas over people. The Logician's creativity will often border on genius; they have a rare ability to see connections that others do not. While they feel they can accomplish anything, INTPs often struggle in personal relationships and may avoid opening up in even their closest relationships.

INTPs can be difficult to speed-read because they are often closed off to even their closest friends. They are likely to appear anti-social and disinterested within social settings. They may fit the stereotype of the "absentminded professor"; brilliant, but completely oblivious to the goings-on around them. They will often pause and look away during conversations so that they can let their wheels turn. They will likely participate in discussions to the extent that they are comfortable and interested. They are also unpreoccupied with appearance and are more likely to dress casually than stylishly. Their affinity for time alone and challenging problems typically draws them to jobs that require them to work long hours. INTPs are also likely to be drawn to computers as both a hobby and a job type.

When interacting with an INTP, be open-minded and ready for change. INTPs are analytically minded but are also never afraid to change course when new information arises. INTPs also enjoy having their problem-solving skills tested; when possible, offer them a creative puzzle or issue they can tackle. This will energize the INTP and may even cause them to let their guard down. Give Logicians space to spin their wheels and come up with a satisfactory solution. Avoid being pushy. The more detail-oriented work that you can spare the INTP from, the better. You can also compliment an INTP on their knowledge and expertise, and they will appreciate it. Being an intensely private person, you should always respect a Logician's privacy.

Challenges may arise between extroverts and INTPs due to the rigors of the INTP's analysis. Extroverts should think carefully about ideas before presenting them to INTPs. Sensors will struggle with the far-reaching vision of the INTP that rarely has anything to do with the present day. INTPs can confuse sensors with their long-winded explanations, and sensors should learn to ask INTPs for clarification. Judgers are likely to have problems keeping INTPs reigned in from exploring new outlets. They should use logic to appeal for INTPs to follow a natural order of things. Feelers will have the most trouble, and when they receive brusque feedback from an INTP they shouldn't take it personally. Feedback from an INTP is often honest and well-thought-out and can prove to be very useful.

Idealists

The intuitive feelers, idealists are similar to conceptualizers in that they both focus on the big picture rather than the day-to-day. Unlike conceptualizers, however, idealists are motivated by people and emotions rather than logic and reason. Idealists put their values and ideals above all else. They value uniqueness and originality over conformity. The life of an idealist is often one long journey of self-discovery and a search for inner meaning.

If you are communicating with someone who you know falls within the idealist temperament, you can use some standard tricks to best talk with them. Idealists are highly empathetic people, and when you appeal to their empathetic nature, they are likely to respond warmly. When you speak passionately about a topic, an idealist is likely to feel your passion and be inspired by it. It is wise to avoid being combative or competitive with an idealist, as they will not respond well to this. Idealists will also appreciate when you speak in terms of personal stories or analogies. They are usually highly creative and imaginative people, so if there is any way you can play to this aspect of their personality, they will respond warmly.

ENFJs

ENFJs are also known as Protagonists. ENFJs strive to always be in harmonious relationships with those around them. Protagonists are lead feelers, and they tend to use this function to always be attuned to the emotions of those around them and try to make them happy. They are perceived by others to be warm, loving, and compassionate. Their knack for people even allows them to anticipate how people are going to feel. Their extroversion allows them to be gifted public speakers, while their feeling function allows them to anticipate what their audience wants. Their least function is thinking, which causes them to struggle when it comes to making logical or objective decisions. When decisions cannot be made using values, ENFJs might become overwhelmed. They are also highly sensitive and may take offense at something that was not intended to offend. Protagonists will idealize relationships which will often lead them to be disappointed in people when they do not live up to the values and expectations of the Protagonist. ENFJs are highly energetic people who feed off others; interactions with others do not wear down ENFJs, but rather give them fuel. ENFJs are good multitaskers and can handle multiple projects on their plate at once. They may become so fixated on completing the many tasks on their plate, that they become inflexible and unreceptive to new information.

ENFJs will give themselves away due to their excellent communication skills. They will hold good eye contact during a conversation. ENFJs will touch people frequently but appropriately, as a way of showing affection. They will lean in when talking to you to show their interest, and their faces are obvious reflections of their emotional state. ENFJs will appear to be experts in both verbal and nonverbal language. They will use both to frequently express their deeply held values and beliefs. They may also ask questions of you that appear personal; ENFJs don't mean to pry, but they enjoy talking about relationships and understanding people on an emotional level. Not only do they excel in large social settings, but their feeler function also allows them to instantly pick up on the emotional climate of a room and act accordingly. They can be very sensitive to criticism and may fear being judged based on their appearance. This usually means ENFJs dress appropriately for the occasion. ENFJs like to take leadership roles and can often be found organizing people or projects.

When talking with an ENFJ, it is important to express your appreciation verbally. ENFJs put a high value on words, and when they receive verbal positive affirmation, they respond warmly. The sensitivity of an ENFJ could lead to them getting their feelings hurt when they receive criticism. Make sure to highlight areas of positivity first, and always give criticism as gently as possible. As lead feelers, it is important that you never diminish the feelings or emotions of an ENFJ, even if they make no logical sense to you. Always try to listen and empathize with a Protagonist rather than criticize. Don't try and confront an ENFJ, as they will seek to avoid confrontation at all costs. It is also essential that you keep your word and not break a commitment to an ENFJ. ENFJs will likely become hurt and disappointed when they are let down by people they care about. You should also attempt to converse with an ENFJ in their manner, use strong eye contact, and address them by their first name.

Introverts won't be able to relate to the constant energy and need for social interaction that the ENFJ exudes. If an extreme introvert is overwhelmed, they should limit time spent around an ENFJ. The best strategy for an introvert is to appreciate an ENFJs rare ability to get them out of their shell. Sensors will likely see ENFJs are too idealistic and unrealistic about their plans. Sensors should try not to overwhelm ENFJs with too many details, and instead let ENFJs continue to thrive in a project manager-like role. Perceivers are more likely to keep an open mind than ENFJs, who will often have blinders on when completing a task. Perceivers can persuade ENFJs by gently expressing the benefits of keeping options open. But be careful, once a perceiver makes a commitment with an ENFJ, they better stick to it! Thinkers represent the biggest gap in personality type with ENFJs. They may see Protagonists as illogical and overly sensitive. They should try not to view an ENFJ as unstable and instead understand that they need to have their emotions respected. Thinkers should take care to be gentle with criticism and not say anything that could be taken as an insult to an ENFJ.

INFJs

INFJs are also referred to as Advocates. INFJs are original thinkers who put a strong value on their personal morals. As lead intuitives, INFJs have a knack for creativity and long-term thinking. They love using their creative skills to help others. They are great at listening to others and empathizing with their feelings. Often soft-spoken people, INFJs are happy working on their creative pursuits behind the scenes and far away from the spotlight. Advocates will try their hardest to keep their close personal relationships in harmony, but at the same time, they value their independence. They are honest and full of integrity, often giving them the ingredients to be inspiring leaders. The INFJ's least function is sensing, which makes them often oblivious to the impracticalities of their vision. They may miss or even ignore key details that could be speed bumps to their vision. Their judger function also makes them incredibly decisive and often dismissive of the ideas of others. This decisiveness along with their determination often makes Advocates extremely productive people. INFJs often plan so big that they run the risk of living in the future and missing out on the joys of the present day. Their strong convictions and values will also lead them to write off a person completely if they feel they have been wronged.

INFJs are sometimes difficult people to get to know. Their introverted function often causes them to hold back in social settings and they will seldom be the life of the party. INFJs would much rather have a one-on-one conversation with you so they can focus their attention on one person. They are known for their great listening skills. You may spot an INFJ listening intently to someone's personal problems and then offering a creative solution. Their verbal and nonverbal language will be reserved, and they will not make overt physical gestures or raise their voice. They will carry themselves with great posture and purpose. When they speak, their language will be thoughtful and deep, often filled with meaning. Advocates are typically formal people who tend to dress more on the conservative side. Their career path will likely involve something that allows them to dream up new ideas or work one-on-one with people. INFJs have deep values, and thus they will likely choose a profession that fits in with those values.

When communicating with an INFJ, you should give them adequate time to think over any proposal before you expect to hear feedback. Advocates would much rather hear about your big vision than about the details of your work, so make sure to present any new ideas in the terms that are most relatable to the Advocate. INFJs also want to hear about how ideas can benefit other people in the future. When you can, express your ideas in a way that shows the utilitarian aspects of your grand plan. INFJs love to toss around creative ideas, problem solve, and illicit feedback, so you should always be game for this when spending time with an INFJ. INFJs might give long-winded explanations, so try your best to be patient. If an INFJ makes you a proposal, it is okay to take your time to think it over; they would do the same in your shoes. As judgers, INFJs are decisive people. Make sure to always meet your deadlines and honor the commitments you make to an INFJ.

Challenges may arise between extroverts and INFJs. While extroverts like to think quickly and speak their mind, INFJs take their time and like to ponder an idea first. Extroverts should try and slow down when communicating with an INFJ and exercise as much patience as possible. Thinkers can fall into the trap of viewing INFJs as too sensitive to other people's emotions. Thinkers should learn to view this side of the INFJ as an asset, as it can give thinkers deeper insight into people. Perceivers are likely to find INFJs to be stubborn and steadfast when they could just as easily be more receptive to other options. Perceivers will find they share common ground in the Advocates love for possibilities. They can play into this love by exploring the many options an Advocate may choose; however, once a path has been chosen, the Advocate is likely to stick to it. INFJs and Sensors will likely butt heads the most. Sensors will be puzzled by the imaginative and mysterious nature of INFJs. Sensors should try and avoid immediately labeling INFJs as impractical and instead appeal to the INFJ's desire to turn their dreams into a tangible result.

ENFPs

ENFPs are also called Campaigners. These extroverted perceivers are driven by endless possibilities. Their lead function is intuition, which gives them an immense understanding of the big picture and how big ideas can best help people. The ENFP's insatiable curiosity leads them to enthusiastically pursue ideas and interests in many fields. ENFPs are fun-loving, quirky, and highly original. Campaigners will often scoff at authority and love to think outside of the box. ENFPs are highly motivated by the belief that anything is possible, and thus they never put a threshold on their dreams. Their least function is sensing, often making them aloof to the details of life and appearing to others as scatterbrained. Their creativity allows them to come up with new ideas constantly, no matter how feasible. More attracted to the idea than the implication, they often will lack the dedication to follow through on their ideas. Their extroversion allows them to build a large network of friends and connections. Campaigners may often call upon their various connections to come together in pursuit of a goal. They are perceptive in regard to people and highly empathetic, giving them excellent powers of persuasion. ENFPs often struggle to work alone. ENFPs are also prone to procrastination due to their inability to make a decision and their susceptibility to distraction. Sometimes overly sensitive, they may become offended and misperceive the intentions of their friends. At times of emotional strife, ENFPs may withdraw and become moody and overwhelmed with life. However, the natural warmth and optimism of an ENFP will allow them to resurface with a fresh outlook on life.

Campaigners can be speed-read by their highly energetic and offbeat mannerisms. Energized by people, a Campaigner will have a large social circle that is varied and often quite diverse. They speak quickly, make jokes frequently, and use their language liberally to entertain people. They will likely speak rapidly and jump from one topic to the next. They have no problem sparking up a conversation with a complete stranger. They will speak their mind, ask a lot of questions, and finish people's sentences. The importance they place on originality will lead them to dress in an irreverent and quirky way. They will usually reserve their deeper emotions to those they are closest with, and with these friends, ENFPs will reveal their sentimentality. Campaigners will often hop from job to job in search of something more creatively stimulating. Their wide range of interests and social groups will always keep the ENFP busy.

When talking with an ENFP, be ready to talk about a wide variety of topics and answer questions as they come. ENFPs will likely lose interest the minute details are discussed, so try and keep things general or on the big picture. ENFPs also love to have their creativity challenged, so do not be afraid to throw radical ideas or possibilities at an ENFP. Campaigners hate the feeling that they are being restricted or controlled, so make sure to present them with as many options as possible. Never shut down their ideas or point out their impracticalities. You should also take care to respect an ENFPs privacy. Although they are extroverted people, they don't enjoy sharing their emotions publicly. As best as you can, try to keep your communication with an ENFP as interesting and fast-paced as possible. Don't attempt to reign in an ENFP with rules or structure because this will only backfire. Give the ENFP enough free reign to be spontaneous and encourage their creative side projects.

ENFPs can prove to be tiresome for many introverts. ENFPs can be loud, quick-talking, and fast-paced in everything they do. Introverts will be able to best communicate with ENFPs on a one-on-one basis. Thinkers will become frustrated at the inconsistent behavior of the ENFP. Thinkers should frame any resistance to the ENFP's behavior in terms of how it can be unfair to others. Judgers will struggle to push ENFPs to make a decision and stick with it. Judgers may find success in getting ENFPs to make a decision by stressing that no decision is permanent. Campaigners will find reassurance in knowing that they are not tied down to any one decision. Sensors will be blown away by the imaginative and off-the-wall style of the ENFP. Sensors should take care not to smother an ENFP's creativity and accept that although an idea may not appear viable to a sensor, an ENFP may see something that they do not.

INFPs

INFPs are often referred to as Mediators. INFPs are on a lifelong pursuit to find meaning and harmony. These lead feelers are governed by their emotions and their own personal values that they set for themselves. INFPs are motivated first and foremost by the need to make sure their actions and morals are in alignment. Their deep-felt beliefs that integrity and honesty are more important than anything will not allow them to pursue something that they do not 100% believe in. The highly empathetic Mediators are deeply sensitive and caring to those they are closest to; however, they choose their inner circle very carefully. To strangers, INFPs can appear cool and aloof due to their shyness. INFPs are often one of the hardest personality types to get to know. The Mediator's least function is thinking, which can often lead to unrealistic behavior and the ability to think objectively. Highly sensitive, INFPs can often get their feelings hurt by others even when there were no ill intentions. Because they are nonconfrontational people, they are likely to let their hurt feelings fester in silence and turn to resentment. INFPs will drop people from their lives when they feel they have been wronged, rather than try and work it out. Highly creative, INFPs are often drawn to the arts and other forms of self-expression. INFPs would much rather chart their own course than follow the crowd. An INFP's main focus is inward, and thus they are often highly spiritual people. They are drawn to quiet time alone where they can read or write.

INFPs are considered to be the most idealistic of the four idealist personality types. When trying to spot an INFP, you might notice an aloofness that suggests that they are not totally present in the moment. Details and mundane activities rarely interest the Mediator. Sometimes perceived by others as impractical, they don't particularly care what others or society thinks they should do, but rather what they feel they should do. They are thoughtful and soft-spoken, and you will rarely see an INFP act aggressive or confrontational. They often have an affinity for writing or poetry. They save their ambition for their own projects, on which they will give their all. INFPs will dress in order to please themselves and not others, thus giving them a unique appearance. While they might appear cold at first, they may open up when someone takes interest in their work.

When communicating with an INFP, remember to keep in mind that they are highly sensitive to criticism and take a lot personally. INFPs are likely to keep their hurt feelings to themselves, so it is best to err on the side of caution before broaching a subject you suspect might offend an INFP. You should also be careful not to dismiss or discount something that the INFP cares about. When you can relate your message or suggestion to something the INFP is passionate about, you are much more likely to get their full attention. Let the Mediator take their time to consider new ideas and then be ready for an in-depth discussion on the implications the idea will have on others. INFPs are invigorated by true passion, so if you can talk about something you are passionate about, the INFP will be genuinely interested. Don't try faking your passion, however, because the INFP will likely be able to tell the difference. You should also respect the INFPs work process, which involves privacy and can change drastically when new information is presented.

Extroverts will likely struggle when attempting to get to know the INFP, and they will likely be shocked at their slow pace of work. Extroverts shouldn't rush an INFP and should instead let an INFP move at their own pace in both relationships and work. Sensors may see INFPs as impractical dreamers. They should take the time to hear out INFPs and their ideas before shutting them down. Judgers may get frustrated at the length it takes INFPs to make a decision. Judgers should present concise options to the INFP and try to set clear deadlines. The less open-ended things are, the more efficient an INFP will behave. Thinkers will feel that they have to walk on eggshells around INFPs due to their sensitivity. They may benefit from testing out edgy ideas on other feelers before presenting them to INFPs.

Words of Caution for Speed Readers

Now that we have gone through the sixteen different personality profiles, you are now much better equipped to read people like a book. Speed-reading is a skill that can be immensely beneficial to almost every social aspect of your life. The more you use it in daily life, the stronger your powers of perception will become. It is important to remember that these sixteen personality profiles are not concrete; no person will fit the description of a personality type with 100% accuracy. The purpose of personality type and speed-reading is not to put people into boxes, but rather to try and understand the intricacies of personalities and their unique communication techniques. Speed-reading gives you a unique ability to empathize with people that you may have once struggled to understand. In this way, speed-reading can be used like a superpower.

Like any superpower, speed-reading should be exercised with caution. You should be prepared for the possibility that people will become defensive when they find out about your speed-reading abilities. Many people do not like to be analyzed, and they may even take offense to the idea that you used your speed-reading skills on them. This can be counterproductive to the whole point of speed-reading: connecting with people. It is important that you downplay your skills. Do not boast about your amazing speed-reading skills and treat it like a parlor game. The minute you begin to use your skills as a cheap trick to impress your friends, it is a safe bet that someone will get their feelings hurt.

Being a speed reader does not make you a mind reader. Don't pretend to know what someone is thinking just because you can identify their personality type. If you insinuate that you know something about a person that they consider intimate and private, you are likely to offend them. It is best to use your skills in a safe and quiet environment. Practice by yourself at first. Hone in your skills through conversations with strangers. The more practice you get, the better you will become.

It is also important to remember that no matter how good you get at speed-reading people, you should never put too much weight on your personality diagnosis. Just because you have figured out a person's personality type, does not mean you will be able to predict behavior or actions. Treat everyone as their own unique individual. Remember, every personality function is a spectrum. No one is 100% introverted or 100% extroverted. You should also always consider the possibility that your personality guess for someone is incorrect. Continue to observe the people you interact with and compile more information on them. The more you know someone, the better you can understand them. Finally, always use speed-reading for honorable reasons. When used correctly, speed-reading can be a beautiful tool for helping you make more memorable and lasting connections with others.

Becoming Fluent in Body Language

We have reached the last chapter of this book. This chapter is designed as a catch-all that will dissect some of the most common body language that you are likely to see on a daily basis. As we have previously discussed, our minds are excellent at subconsciously picking up on body language, but we rarely consciously register it. The next time you are at an office meeting, job interview, family gathering, first date, or social gathering, keep an eye out for these common body language tics.

The Hands

The hands are essential human tools not just for accomplishing tasks but for nonverbal communication. Think of how a police officer might yell at a criminal and tell them to "show their hands," in order to prove they are unarmed. When someone testifies in court, they put one palm on a bible and hold the other palm up for everyone to see. When Americans say the Pledge of Allegiance or sing the national anthem, they will hold a hand over their heart. These cultural norms of body language are significant because they deliver a message that everyone understands.

Hands are often used as tools to relay honesty or deceit. It is commonly understood that open palms indicate openness. If someone is pleading with you to believe them, and they are coming to you with open arms and open palms, they are likely telling the truth. Open palms are the body's way of subconsciously showing that it has nothing to hide. Conversely, hidden palms could be a sign of deceit. If someone is hiding their palms by putting their hands in their pockets, or crossing their arms over their chest, this could be a signal that they are hiding something.

The palm has immense power when it comes to delivering a nonverbal message. You can speak in the exact same vocal tone and say the exact same words, but if you switch up your palm position, it is likely the person you are talking to will receive a completely different message. A palm-up hand gesture is a submissive or pleading gesture that is often used in a nonthreatening manner. Think of this gesture as the equivalent of a beggar asking for money on a street corner. The palm-down gesture is much more threatening and is used to project authority and dominance. Asking someone to do something with a palm-down gesture will likely come off as more of a demand than a request. The person you are talking to may also begin to have antagonist feelings toward the request, as no one likes to feel like they are being bossed around. But the worst hand gesture you can use when talking to someone is the palm-closed, finger-pointed hand gesture. This gesture is interpreted by the listener as an attempt to beat the listener into submission. Humans are naturally repelled by this hand gesture and are likely to find it aggressive, annoying, and off-putting.

One of the most important exchanges of body language is the handshake. Most often used in business settings and during introductions, the handshake is a greeting of direct physical contact. A handshake can also have direct implications in terms of the relationship of the two parties shaking hands. Similar to the palm gestures, the way in which someone positions their palm when they shake your hand will often signify their intentions and how they view their relationship with you. If someone turns their palm downward in a handshake, this is a sign of dominance, and you might subconsciously grow cautious. If someone turns their palms upward during a handshake, they are submitting to you, and you may be convinced that you can persuade this person easily. An equitable handshake is when both palms are in a vertical position. This is likely to put both shakers at ease and make them feel comfortable with the encounter.

When conversing or listening to people, it is always a good idea to watch their hands. People are prone to speaking with their hands, and oftentimes they may reveal something with their hands that their words are hiding. When someone summarizes two sides of an argument, they may describe one side of the argument while using one hand, and describe the other side with the other hand. "On the other hand," they may say. In scenarios like this, both right-handed and left-handed people will use their dominant hand when speaking about their preferred viewpoint. Hand gestures are equally effective when using them to deliver a message. As we have discussed, nonverbal communication is far more impactful than simple verbal communication. When you incorporate powerful hand gestures into a speech or story, studies have found that the audience is much more likely to recall the content of your words.

Many common hand gestures are recognizable due to their common use within culture. The rubbing of two palms together is often used as a signal of positive anticipation. This common hand gesture can change connotations depending on the speed at which the palms are rubbed together. A slow and methodical palm rub is likely indicated that someone foresees a positive outcome for themselves, while a faster palm rub indicates anticipation for others to be positively impacted. Rubbing an index finger and thumb together is another popular hand gesture. This gesture is often used to relay an expectancy of money. It is a good idea to avoid using this thumb and index finger gesture when in business meetings or sales pitches. This gesture may carry negative connotations about money and could be taken the wrong way by a business colleague.

When someone clenches their hands together, they are likely holding back frustrations. Hands clenched together is a common gesture of someone who is hiding an anxious or negative attitude. Researchers who studied body language within negotiations found that the clenched-hands gesture came up a lot. Most often the clenched hands were a sign that someone felt that they were losing the negotiation, or that they were struggling to get someone to see their point of view. A distant cousin to the clenched hands is the hand steeple, in which the fingertips of one hand will lightly press against the other to form a makeshift "steeple." This is often a symbol of confidence and is most likely to be seen when a superior is talking with a subordinate. Pressing the hands completely together can even be an unconscious attempt to appear godlike. The steeple should not be used in a context where you are trying to be persuasive, because you run the risk of coming off as arrogant.

Another powerful hand gesture that exudes confidence is the act of putting your hands behind your back. Using one hand to hold the other hand behind the back is a common hand gesture of authority figures. By holding their arms and hands behind their back, a person is leaving their vulnerable front areas completely exposed to oncoming threats. This symbolizes fearlessness in those who observe the gesture. This hand gesture is often clustered with the rocking on the balls of the feet—an attempt to achieve greater height.

Perhaps the most distinctive part of the hand that is used in body language is the thumb. Thumbs are thought to represent strength of character and ego. A man who wants to convey confidence and authority is likely to display his thumbs for those around him to see. One of the most popular gestures of this kind is putting the hands in the pockets while leaving the thumbs protruding out. The display of thumbs can also be clustered with an arms-crossed gesture, in which the fingers are tucked under the arms, and the thumbs are stuck up in the air. This gesture signals a closed-off mindset (crossed arms) as well as a superior or confident attitude (thumb display). Gesturing at someone with a thumb when speaking about them can be interpreted as a sign of ridicule. Because people see thumbs as a way to exude authority, using thumbs to speak to people may reveal your true feelings of superiority.

Smiles and Laughs

As we discussed in the section on first impressions, a well-timed smile is a great way to charm someone and put them at ease. Two muscle groups control the human smile: the zygomatic major muscles and the orbicularis oculi. The zygomatic major muscles run down the face and connect to the corners of the mouth, while the orbicularis oculi pull the eyes back. The important distinction between the two is that the zygomatic major muscles are consciously controlled, meaning a smile strictly from the mouth can be faked. The orbicularis oculi muscles act independently. When someone smiles with wrinkles behind their eyes, they are giving you a genuine smile that was completely involuntary.

In terms of body language, smiling and laughter are universally understood to indicate that a person is happy. However, a smile can also have more subtle connotations. A smile can also be a sign of submission. Chimpanzees use their smiles to indicate two things: that they are fearful of another chimp, or that they are not a threat. In similar ways, human beings will often smile at others as a sign that they are not a threat. When you smile at a stranger, you are offering them the opportunity to accept you on a personal level. This stranger might smile back to signify that you are on an equal playing field, or they may withhold a return smile, which would be an attempt to signify dominance over you. Classic Hollywood tough guys like Clint Eastwood and Charles Bronson made careers from their patented lack of smiling. To men like Clint and Charles, to smile would be a sign of weakness, which their characters couldn't afford to show in the movies.

This is not to say that you should avoid smiling so that you do not appear weak. In general, it is a great practice to smile as often as possible in social settings. Science has proven that smiling is contagious, and when you smile it has an unavoidable positive effect on your mood. Thus, your smile is likely to rub off on people and give them a positive feeling associated with you. Smiling is an excellent piece of body language that will work in your favor.

Similar to smiling, laughter is a piece of body language that has far-ranging benefits. Laughter is almost always attractive to others. The more you laugh, the more people you will attract to your circle, and the more friends you will make. Laughter is also extremely good for your well-being. Laughter causes the breath to quicken, which in turn exercises the diaphragm, stomach, face, neck, and shoulders. There is also a resulting increase of oxygen into the bloodstream which increases circulation. Other benefits of laughter include burning calories, stimulating appetite, dilating the arteries, and lowering the heart rate. Laughter also engages endorphins, the body's natural painkillers.

Laughter and smiles are the easiest way to use your body language to make a great impression on someone. When people share a laugh, they have immediately shared a bond. The positive emotions that are associated with smiles and laughter are often connected to the people with who we share them.

The Arms

The arms can act as one of the most expressive parts of the body. When reading body language, it is important to closely examine the placement of a person's arms. Arms are most often used to create a barrier between yourself and those you interact with. Conversely, they can be used to express openness.

The crossed arm position is perhaps the most well-known and recognizable piece of body language. Crossing your arms is a subconscious attempt to protect yourself. At its most primal level, when someone crosses their arms, it could be because they sense an imminent threat. Crossed arms could also be a subconscious reveal that someone is disinterested or untrusting of the person who is speaking. Studies have shown that people who cross their arms while attempting to learn new information are much less likely to retain the new information. This indicates that in a similar way as smiling tricks your brain into being happy, crossing your arms tricks your brain into closing itself off to new information.

If you are attempting to make a good impression on someone, don't let yourself cross your arms in the middle of a conversation. While it might be the exact opposite of your intention, people are likely to see crossed arms as a sign that you are disinterested. You may feel that crossing your arms is a comfortable position, and you mean no offense by the gesture. Ironically, body language will feel most comfortable when it corresponds to your attitude. Whether you are conscious of it or not, it is best to avoid the gesture in social settings. Body language is a crucial means of communication, and the meaning of the message is determined just as much by the receiver as it is by the sender.

Perhaps you are in a business meeting or a sales pitch, and the person you are speaking to is holding a crossed-armed position. Knowing that this position will subconsciously cause this person to be less receptive to your messaging, you feel you are in trouble. What can you do to make the person more receptive? You could give the person something to hold. A brochure, pitch deck, pen, questionnaire, or writing sample is a great way to get people to open up their arms and lean forward. Unbeknownst to the person you are pitching to, you have just primed them to bring a more open attitude to your meeting.

Various cross-armed body language clusters reveal more specific feelings. A person exhibiting crossed arms with clenched fists is most likely angry and even hostile. This body language accompanied by a tight-lipped smile or clenched teeth could be a sign of an incoming physical attack. Respond to this type of body language cautiously, as this person is likely in an aggressive state of mind. Another common cluster is the cross-armed stance with the double-arm-grip. This body language is a form of self-comfort, similar to giving yourself a hug. You might spot this body language in a hospital waiting room or on a turbulent flight. It can also be a sign of insecurity. If someone is not buying what you are selling, they may very well show you the double-arm-grip.

One part of the arm, in particular, is highly susceptible to nonverbal exchanges: the elbow. Believe it or not, a simple elbow touch can be a powerfully positive nonverbal exchange. The next time you are participating in an introductory handshake, lightly place your left hand on the person's right elbow. Studies have shown that this simple elbow touch can work wonders to make a positive impression. One such study was known as "The Phone Booth Test." Experimenters left a coin in a phone booth, and once a person walked in and found the coin, the experimenter returned to the booth to ask if the person had found a coin. Only 23% of people admitted to experimenters that they had found a coin. However, when the experimenter touched the person's elbow for a mere three seconds, a remarkable 68% of people admitted they had found the coin and returned it. Elbows are not considered private parts of the body, and thus people are rarely offended by being touched there. Oddly enough, while touching a stranger is not necessarily acceptable behavior, the rareness of the experience creates an impression in the person whose elbow is touched. Also, physical contact creates a momentary bond between two people, usually unconscious. It is important not to overstay your welcome when you touch someone's elbow; three seconds should be the maximum amount of time you hold the touch.

The Eyes

The eyes are one of our most powerful tools of communication. The amount of eye contact in a conversation will help to govern the flow and length of the conversation. The reason such phrases as "icy stare," "inviting eyes," or "evil eye" have become such popular expressions is because people understand how much impact the eyes have on nonverbal exchanges. You may also be familiar with the expression that "the eyes are windows into the soul." In many ways, this is true. A person's pupils will often reveal their true emotions, and they operate completely outside of conscious control.

Watching a person's pupils is an excellent way to spot their current mood. People's pupils can dilate up to four times larger when their attitude becomes excited. Dilated pupils can be a sign of sexual attraction, as they are sometimes referred to as "bedroom eyes." Conversely, when a person begins to feel a negative mood such as anger, their pupils will contract into very small and "beady" eyes. As humans, we are naturally attracted to dilated pupils. You are likely to find a person with dilated pupils warm and welcoming, while you might see a person with contracted pupils as cold or threatening. Studies have shown that pupils are dilated when you are exposed to anything that you find pleasing, including pictures of attractive people, good food, politicians you support, or music you enjoy. In many ways, pupils are indicators of a person's level of pleasure in the current moment. One thing to be conscious of is that pupils also change size depending on lighting conditions. This is why many successful romantic encounters occur in dimly lit places: people's pupils dilate in darker lighting conditions, giving the impression that two people are interested in each other.

Another common piece of body language is the eyebrow raise. This is often used as a form of a long-distance "hello," in most cultures. When used rapidly, the eyebrow raise can also be an unconscious reaction of surprise; oftentimes a way to acknowledge someone's presence. You are not likely to eyebrow flash a stranger, as they might perceive this as you insinuating that you know each other. Likewise, if someone you meet does not raise their eyebrows, this could be perceived as a potentially threatening gesture. The eyebrow flash is a great way to spark up a conversation or to indicate that you like someone. This is a welcoming piece of body language and can be used liberally and often with positive results. However, you should be aware that intentionally raised eyebrows is seen as a sign of submission. If you were looking to appear intimidating or assert dominance, you would likely lower your eyebrows.

Body language clusters around the eyes are often used within human mating rituals. There are many clusters that are standardly used by women in order to appear attractive to men. A cluster that includes lowering the head and looking up is a way for a woman to appear submissive and childlike. Because this cluster evokes both paternal and maternal feelings in others, it can be a great gesture for garnering sympathy. Another common cluster used in mating situations is the lowering of eyelids, raising of the eyebrows, and parting of the lips. This is a hypersexual look for a female to give a male, and it can also suggest mystery and secretiveness. When a woman is attempting to get the attention of a man in a public place, she will often meet his gaze for roughly two seconds, and then look down and away (in a sign of submission). Studies have shown that because most men will not pick up on this gaze the first time, women will have to meet a man's gaze an average of three times to successfully deliver their intended message. Similarly, the sideways glance paired with an eyebrow raise is a way to indicate your attraction to someone and can be used by either sex.

Certain eye signals can be used to indicate disinterest. If you notice that someone is blinking frequently this could be a sign that they are no longer interested in conversing with you. Frequent blinking is the brain's unconscious way of removing you from their sight because they are either bored, disinterested, or feel superior to you. The longer a blink is held, the more intense a person's feelings of disinterest. If you suspect the blinking is part of a superiority complex, keep an eye out for the blinking to be coupled with a look down the nose. When someone tilts their head back and gives the appearance that they are looking down their nose at you, this is a good indicator that you have taken a misstep in your conversation, and you would be wise to change course. Another common eye gesture is the darting eyes. Darting eyes seem to suggest a nervous energy. When eyes dart around mid-conversation, this is due to the brain subconsciously looking for escape routes.

Summary

If this book has properly served its purpose, you will have acquired useable and relevant information for reading people. Ideally, you can return to this book and use it as a reference as you continue to practice your skills of social perception.

First, we established the most important practice that should be apparent in every aspect of your speed-reading practice: empathy. Humans are emotional beings who crave connection. Leading with empathy is not only a huge part of understanding how people behave, but it is also an incredibly attractive quality for a spouse, employee, friend, or conversationalist to have. People that are attuned to their own emotions, as well as the emotions of others, are said to be high in emotional intelligence. The emotional intelligence paradigm includes four parts: self-awareness, self-management, social awareness, and relationship management. Working on each of these aspects of emotional intelligence can help a person to become better emotionally adjusted and to make stronger impressions on those around them.

Next, the Myers-Briggs Type Indicator serves as a strong framework for the speed-reading skills that are taught in this book. The sixteen Myers-Briggs personality types are identified by how they fall on four spectrums: how people are energized (extrovert or introvert), the kind of information they pay attention to (sensor or intuitive), how they make decisions (feelers or thinkers), and how they like to organize the world (judgers or perceivers). While the Myers-Briggs personality indexes should not be considered to be written in stone, they can be used as a helpful tool for differentiating the personality traits we see in people. The sixteen types can also be broken out into four temperaments: the traditionalists, the experiencers, the conceptualizers, and the idealists. When you can accurately place someone into the correct temperament category, you will be at a great starting point to understand how this person views the world, makes decisions, and interacts with others.

We then covered how we can become better equipped to speed-read people through the art of observation. Perception and observation are skills that can be refined and improved upon, just like any other. With practice, our minds can be taught how to catalog as much information as possible in any given situation. We can learn what questions to ask, what to look for, and how to avoid making assumptions. There is much to be learned about observation through the practice of studying art. Art is subjective, suggestive, and often opaque. Yet answers that are hidden from plain sight can be deduced by looking at mysterious pieces of art and asking questions such as *who*, *what*, *when*, and *where*? The human brain can't fathom the amount of information that is overlooked in our daily lives. When we begin to practice, we can learn to step back and notice things that everyone else misses.

Next, we dove into the body language that is often associated with liars. It is important to remember that every human lies and that all liars, even the great ones, have tells. The best thing that you can do when attempting to spot a liar is to be an active listener. Liars will often bury themselves when you let them talk. Exercising your observation skills when conversing with a suspected liar is all you need to detect a fibber. Oftentimes liars will reveal themselves through their body language, where their body language will be incongruent with the words that they are saying. There are also common speech patterns that are favorite strategies of liars such as bullying, lying by omission, or qualifying their virtue. Once you have developed the proper skills to spot a lie, it is pivotal that you remember not to take it personally. Most lies are little white lies that have very little negative impact. Use your speed-reading skills to identify lies and then learn more about the person by noticing what they lie about.

Then we went through strategies that can lead to successful conversations. While speed-reading is often associated with observation and perception, conversations are often the arena in which speed readers will be put to the test. Being able to accurately read someone doesn't offer many benefits if you can't successfully communicate with said person. It is essential that you make a strong first impression in any new conversation. Keep strong eye contact, have a firm handshake, and smile as often as you can. The most important tool in any conversationalist toolkit is asking questions. Try to ask open-ended questions that give the other person a chance to talk about themselves. Once a conversation begins to go well and a rapport is built, the person will begin to feel that a connection has been made. People are also naturally attracted to people that act, behave, and speak like them. Using techniques such as synchronization and mirroring, you can subconsciously suggest to the person you are talking to that you are like them. This can help turn any conversation into a meaningful connection.

Next, we broke down the sixteen personality types in the Myers-Briggs index. By studying the profiles of the sixteen types, you can get a better understanding of how human beings behave. People of different personality types dress, socialize, work, speak, and behave differently. There are certain tics and mannerisms that might tip you off toward someone's personality type, or at least their temperament. Once you have a good idea of someone's personality type, you can more easily converse with them and have more effective interactions. You don't have to know a person's exact personality type to improve your communications. If you can tell whether a person is an extrovert or introvert, you will understand whether the person feels the need to converse constantly, or if they feel more comfortable with periods of quiet. If you can spot a feeler from a thinker, you will know whether an appeal to someone's emotions will be more effective than an appeal using logic. It is important to use your skills as a speed reader modestly and not to showboat. Use speed-reading empathetically, and you will find it has many benefits to you and those you interact with.

Finally, we discussed some common body language gestures that you will regularly see. The way we shake hands, hold our arms, and divert our eyes can all be unintentionally revealing how we feel. The body can often be a looking glass into the subconscious motivations and feelings of the individual. By learning how to study the body and spot different body language clusters when they occur, you will soon be able to quickly recognize common clusters.

In the introduction, a strange man approached you on the street and claimed to be a mind reader. He effectively read your body language and determined the emotions and motivations you were feeling at any given moment. So, the question remains, is reading body language equivalent to being a mind reader? Of course not. No human being is identical. No matter how observant you are at picking up body language clusters, how high you rank in emotional intelligence, or how skilled you are at spotting personality types, you will never be a mind reader. There is no magic involved in this process. The skills taught in this book, the skills that you have hopefully developed, are not cheat codes, but rather performance enhancers. If you apply them right, you will become a better communicator, an excellent reader of people, and a more empathetic individual. At the end of the day, this is all anyone can hope for. Good luck and get busy speed-reading.

Made in the USA
Middletown, DE
03 October 2021

49529226R00086